Gold Man Review

Gold Man Review is published once a year by Gold Man Publishing in Salem, Oregon.

Subscriptions available at www.goldmanpublishing.com

The editors invite submissions of previously unpublished works of fiction, nonfiction, poetry, art, and photography. Manuscripts, photographs, and art work can be submitted at www.goldmanpublishing.com

Copyright 2011/2012 Gold Man Publishing / Gold Man Review LLC.
PO Box 8202, Salem, OR 97303
Printed by Gold Man Publishing
ISSN: 2162-8238
ISBN: 978-0-615-54935-4

No part of this work may be reproduced or transmitted in any form or by any means, electronical or mechanical, including but not limited to photocopying and recording, or by any other information storage or retrieval system without proper written permission of the publisher. Address all requests to Permissions, Gold Man Publishing, PO Box 8202, Salem, OR 97303.

Contents

Daniel Chan: *Lois Rosen* 1

One Day at Antietam: *Mark Russell Reed* 2

Fall on the Willamette: *John Byrne* 5

The Tale of a Twisted Rye: *Mark W. McIntire* 6

Negative Space: *Isaiah Swan* 7

The Secret of Me: *Nyla Alisia* 11

An Interview with Naseem Rakha 12

Sands of Oman: *Naseem Rakha* 20

The Housewife's Tale: *Monica Storss* 22

Shadows of Evenfall: *Nyla Alisia* 23

In the Irish Countryside: *F.I. Goldhaber* 24

Animal Souls: *Brigitte R.C. Goetze* 25

Gray: *Ariel* 26

Life and Death and Flies: *Heather Cuthbertson* 28

Ballet: *Nicklas Roetto* 34

Postcards from Iraq: *Nicklas Roetto* 35

Hotel Beloved: *Tim Pfau* 38

In the Room There is a Painting: *Marc Janssen* 40

An Interview with Lisa Schroeder 41

Reading Lillie: *Jean Rover* 46

No Man's Land: *Lois Rosen* 50

Freedom Walk: *Samuel Hall* 51

Vertigo: *Melanie Patterson* 55

Panis Angelicus: *Michael M. Pacheco* 56

Reflection: *Danny Earl Simmons* 61

A Wagging Tale About Wagging Tales: G.R. *Vince Johnson* 62

The Voice of the Turtle is Heard in Our Land: *Bob Gersztyn* 64

Hand Colored Image of John Fahey in Front of the Senator Hotel Ruins, circa 1997: *Bob Gersztyn* 69

Working for the State: *Ariel* 70

Sold: *Darren Howard* 71

Arrows: *Monica Storss* 74

To Know Too Much: *Frank Yates* 75

Noteworthy Event: *Kathleen Saviers* 76

Displaced: *Nyla Alisia* 80

Kalends of September: *Stephen Eichner* 82

Un Marché á Tunis: *Mark W. McIntire* 86

An Interview with Gina Ochsner 87

Two Prophets: *Mark Russell Reed* 93

Yesterday's News: *Nyla Alisia* 96

Rosehips: *Brigitte R.C. Goetze* 97

Eskimo Kiss: *M.S. Ebbs* 98

Love Sucks cc: Mary Howitt: *Heather Cuthbertson* 99

Nonfiction Love: *Joe Donovan* 102

Water Soluble: *Bethany Williams* 106

Middle School Sway: *Danny Earl Simmons* 108

Conversations with My Mother's Purse: *F.I. Goldhaber* 109

One Snowy Night: *Sandra M. McDow* 110

Their Song: *Lois Rosen* 112

Traveling Companions: *Mark W. McIntire* 115

Future: *Nyla Alisia* 116

Meet the Contributors 117

Advertising 121

Illustration by Kaitrin Bassett

Letter from the Editors

Gold Man Review Issue I has been a hero's journey.

We heeded the call to adventure and left the safety of the ordinary world. When the road proved bumpy, uphill, and bordering along a steep precipice, we doubted the call and doubled back. Mentors appeared and we studied their work, giving us the confidence to press forward and cross the first threshold. We gathered allies and discovered challenges, but we faced every test and marched on, coming ever closer to accomplishing our goal. We fought battles, both large and small; each threatened to crush our mettle, but we overcame. With blue pencils in hand, we braved the road again, traveling further and further until we overtook the Shadow of Failure and destroyed it. Weary, scarred, and homesick, we returned.

The work herein is the product of our journey. The elixir brought back to the ordinary world. The gift we share wrought with themes of faith, love, and strife.

Until the next journey,

Editor-in-Chief
Heather Cuthbertson

Executive Editor
Marilyn Ebbs

Editor
Darren Howard

Editor
Samuel Hall

Project Editor
Nicklas Roetto

Editor
Mark Russell Reed

Assistant Editor
Rachel Lofton

Assistant Editor
Mary-Gray Mahoney

Daniel Chan
Lois Rosen

I read your name Page One four straight days,
watched Internet clips of the slashed
taxi driver, burned parishioners, police.
It couldn't be. But it was, the man who
spoke little in ESL classes, but won
college writing contests. Reporters don't have
stories I saved of your fleeing China. *Visions*,
the college journal, published one in 1996. 2006,
you sloshed flaming gasoline in People's Church.
Coats ignited, flames singed a woman's neck.
Congregants tackled you, published letters
praying for your soul. Paranoid schizophrenic.
1989, you drowned your daughter, spent five
years at the State Hospital. Pills must have quelled
your voices days you attended class.
I remember your slight smile, chubby cheeks.
Do you remember me? Better you don't
or I could have been the one in flames.
One student, who saw you a week before
the attack, said that as you spoke, your hands
shook. Daniel, dear student, I never imagined
the State Hospital released you, "a model patient."
Now they'll lock you up for good. I saved
your photo.

One Day at Antietam
Mark Russell Reed

Bud had participated in the annual reenactment of the Battle of Antietam for the last 16 years. He had his own flintlock rifle and uniform. The latter was getting a bit threadbare and moth-eaten (his current wife wasn't much for sewing), but he felt this added realism. It was realism that he and the rest of his "regiment"—all long-time participants—most prided themselves on, even to the point of abstaining from canned beer on the morning of the reenactment. They opted instead for bourbon made in the time-honored sour mash method.

In particular, they prided themselves on their mock deaths, especially important because their regiment was to fall during the initial charge. They didn't cushion their landings; they were tough men and a bruise or two was the least they could suffer when their forebears had died for freedom. Neither were they overly theatrical; for a generation that hadn't known battle themselves, sandwiched between Vietnam and Iraq, they mimicked getting shot with an almost uncanny naturalism. Whether this was aided by or in spite of the bourbon was a matter for speculation, especially by neighboring regiments, who had genuine respect for their art.

Bud himself was something of a star in this regard. While some men clutched at their chests and fell to their knees the same way each year, and others rehearsed beforehand a slight variation on last year's fall, Bud fell a different way each time, unplanned and spontaneous. His technique, he said, was "to get in the spirit and go with the flow." He might have said there was something Zen to his approach, if he'd had more familiarity with the word.

His fall this year didn't disappoint. By a certain standard it was his best ever, for he truly tapped into the spirit of the thing. His motions were a perfectly precise duplication of a soldier who'd been shot and fallen on that exact spot. And as Bud hit the ground, he became aware of an intense searing pain in his gut.

Recovering from the initial shock, he quickly became aware of some other things—the horrible groaning of the men around him, the painful screams of other men not far away, and not least of all, the blood.

In the same place, but some time away, Pvt. Isaiah Nelson was realizing that in an instant his pain had vanished. Then he became aware of a curious sensation in his body, one which in his short life he'd experienced few times, and which in this context he couldn't identify at all—the liquor in his veins. The whole atmosphere and feeling of the place was different in a way he couldn't define. He looked up at the sky, which was clear and blue. A bird flew overhead. I must be in Heaven, he thought.

He continued to lie there, staring at the sky and feeling the buzz. After a time, the fallen men around him began to get up. They laughed heartily, shook hands, and slapped each other on the back. It was a scene more befitting of Vikings entering Valhalla than Christians entering Paradise, but he wasn't in a state to question things.

"Nelson!" said a voice above him. That was the name written in ink on his uniform; the group represented an actual regiment, and on that day they referred to one another by the names of real soldiers. "You clown, get up."

Nelson accepted the hand held out to assist him and rose slowly. Across the battlefield, every man was getting up, dusting himself off, and smiling. Not one displayed evidence of a wound or injury. In the distance people clapped and cheered.

His group had gathered their things and now began to head back. He went to fall in with them, wondering what awaited them on the other side of the tree line, when someone said, "Hey! Don't forget your rifle."

He looked back at it on the ground. Why would I want it now? he wondered. Then he looked across the field again and it struck him that it was a beautiful place. He couldn't leave a gun lying here.

Bud was having much the opposite experience. He caught on quickly enough that the world around him was that of 1862, but after being dragged to the medical tent, he formed a new hypothesis. I am in Hell.

He had no great delusions about the nature of 19th-century battlefield medicine, but now that he was living it—experiencing the pain and the screams and the stench and the slow violence, and in so immediate a way—he was sure this was some kind of infernal parody, an intensification of the real thing. Somehow he'd died and an infinitely cruel and horrible netherworld of torment had been mockingly designed after the scene of his death. That much seemed obvious.

Mark Russell Reed

The reenactors made their way to the parking lot. The men held their Ford pick-ups in high esteem, but they weren't exactly chariots of the gods. It was this that first gave Pvt. Nelson real pause. He was expecting an angel to guide him to his eternal home. At least a tunnel of light. He watched all the others drive away—with amazing speed, to be sure, but also a lot of noise and belching of smoke. Leaving in small groups, they seemed to fan out, dispersing widely. Wherever they went, none seemed hesitant how to get there. Finally left alone, Nelson felt no compulsion to try the last remaining truck.

As sure as Bud was that this was his final damnation, he trusted in his survival instinct, which meant treating his wounds himself. He had some brief medical training from his stint as a volunteer fireman, and as dim as his memory of it was, he was certain it was better than the alternative. He did what he could, while spending most of the long evening fighting off surgeons, assistants, and anyone else who tried to approach him.

Over the course of their respective, parallel nights, both men succumbed to sleep, and as they dreamed, returned to their rightful bodies, so that it was only as dreams they would understand their experiences. The greater part of their wonder was at the states they woke to and what it might say of their deeper natures—Pvt. Nelson as the lone survivor, for the moment, of his regiment, Bud still in the park, next to a burned-out campfire and the remains of a roasted squirrel.

Fall on the Willamette
John Byrne

           Small shadows
               Dart
        From the river's bank
To trace the lunge, swoop, tumble twist, turn
         Of wind-borne leaves
      Upon the mirror surface of
           The water flow
              Until
           Unerringly
           Each meets
            Its leaf's
            Descent
           And they
           Together
             Float
             Away

The Tale of a Twisted Rye
Mark W. McIntire

The wry gypsy gentleman
Cockeyed kerchief on his head
Drained his glass of whiskey
Ignored the crust of bread, he
Poked at an errant caraway
Then leaned over to one side

Arthritic elbows creaked
As he began to rise.
Taking up a twisted whangee
Like some Sri Lankan raj
He angled out into the day
Astray in a mirage.

Negative Space
Isaiah Swan

I take the check and order number from the cashier behind the counter, the one with the half-dry grease spot around the nametag on his shirt and the random epiphany that he's just now noticed I'm there. The order number, 42, is emblazoned in a bold font on one of those plastic triangles that the cashier reminds me to put at the edge of the table. This is the only fast food place around here where somebody brings the food. It seems pretentious almost. It's fast food that's not really fast food because the fast food is brought to the table. Customer service, good old-fashioned family values, because we care. And then I get the plastic tray and peel back the thin tissue holding the burger together and the bun's squashed flat and the two pickles are all on one side and the real beef patty is 6 millimeters thick. But it still tastes better than any other chain and I guess that's good enough for me.

 I eat alone. When I'm here I always eat alone. I don't mind, though. I don't mind. I like to watch. People. All these people. Absorbing them. Breathing them in. The next customer orders a double cheeseburger and mocha milkshake and the cashier gives him that same nonexistent expression.

 Empty parking spot,
 one-way mirror,
 negative space,
 between the proton and electron.

 The customer doesn't notice and stands by the condiment bar tiled in roll-out plastic and waits for the guy on kitchen duty to take the time to set his food in the paper bag and the paper bag on the counter and read off the order number into the wire-thin microphone next to the register.

 He just stands there, foot tapping, arms crossed, head down, glancing every few seconds at the watch on his right arm tucked into his left but I can tell he's got nowhere to go. He's just checking so he looks like he's here only because he's going to be somewhere better within the space of 15 minutes. He stands there in new jeans, a plaid shirt with the top button undone, and his polished watch hoping everyone assumes he's off to a new café downtown where a girl with a simple ponytail of clean hair and a long-sleeved shirt holds a guitar gently across her leg, running her fingers down each string like there's nothing else in the world but her and that worn guitar, that resilient string and she wouldn't have it any other way and he'll be the only one to walk up to her as she carefully packs away her guitar in a hard case with faded velvet, a tear in the side and tell her how much he liked that song she wrote yesterday about the bluebird on the park bench and get the only smile she gives tonight that isn't her guitar's. But all he's going to do is open his apartment door, toss the empty bag into the garbage can under the sink, and drop onto the couch he got from the friend that moved away sometime last year, sit in front of the blank TV screen, looking ahead. In front of him. Somewhere.

It's not all that dreary though. There's a little girl in the corner. Her older sister just bangs the unarticulated doll that came with the box of chicken nuggets on the table. But the little girl, she's going to be a scientist or something someday. I can see it by the way she scrunches down in her seat and peers across the top of her blackened patty, the burger upside-down, the bottom bun carefully placed beside the untouched milk carton, 2%. Her eyes are level with the burger and I can tell she's thinking about the way the burger's so much bigger when examined in detail, the way the bumps in the meat make the bottom of the patty not actually a planar surface, the way a circle is a line when all that is visible is the one side. The older sister bends the doll's arm back while telling her parents about her teacher that gets so angry all the time while the parents talk about the president and Stephen King in between polite nods. But the smaller girl doesn't even look at them as she methodically pries the patty from the other bun making sure not to tear the barely-melted cheese. Doesn't even seem to know they're there.

She's going to graduate top of her class from a good school on the East Coast, not Ivy League but good enough, someplace she still has to work, and she's going to be snatched up by a grad school instantly, given a full ride because of the quality of her undergrad work on degenerative disease. Twenty-six years from now, she's going to get a Nobel Prize for finding a cure for Parkinson's and I'm going to see her acceptance speech and laugh and tell my kids I saw her when she was a little girl eating a burger in a fast food restaurant a few streets away from where I used to live just after I'd graduated from college and I'll tell them how she pried the patty off her bun and didn't tear the cheese.

A girl, one of the food-baggers from the kitchen behind the counter, walks out with a tray that has a single burger and a cup of iceless water and sits two tables over and doesn't look around at all. This is the place she lives in every day and she sits there and unwraps her single-patty burger and everyone's an object, a piece of furniture, and I'm a—.

She unwraps her burger and she has an expression, a tired sort of look, worn like a ragged bathrobe and when she gets home she's not even going to take off her uniform or hat before she slumps on the couch and falls asleep with her arms splayed out by her legs and her mouth open, her crumpled hair running out of her hat and tangled around her ears.

She starts eating, not looking up, bent over the tray, leaning on both elbows resting on the edge of the table, barely holding her rounded shoulders curving over her food, a tight ridge running along her shoulder and I want to reach out and brush it. Just feel it give.

A braver man might try to start a conversation. Not braver. A different man. A different man might try to talk to her, might just go over and lean toward her and try to talk to her and she would look up and tell him she's just trying to eat her burger that's the only thing she's eaten all day and let this day wash over her in as forgettable a way as possible so if you really want to save me would you please just leave me alone and we'll all be happier, thank you. But he wouldn't leave it alone, being rejected doesn't hurt half as much as understanding there's nothing you can do when there are some places in this world you'll never be able to reach.

So he'll keep trying to talk to her and she'd get angry but she wouldn't be able to shut him down because her boss can hear and if this gets out of hand she'll lose the only job she'll ever be able to find in this economy. When it gets to the point it is clear he'll never leave her alone, he is past the point of no return, that's when I'll stand and walk over and ask him what are you doing hitting on my girlfriend or maybe just stand over him and tell him it's a lost cause and everyone here can hear what a jackass you're making of yourself so leave her alone, and he'll get flustered and stammer and apologize and walk out of the restaurant as fast as he can, walk out, head down, hands in his pockets and she'll look up.

She will look at me, smile, her little wisps of hair will play around her forehead, and she'll say thank you and I'll return the smile, nod, and go back to my seat.

She finishes and puts her tray almost gently on top of the garbage receptacle and goes back behind the counter to take the register so the guy with the stain on his collar can take his smoking break out back and I'm chewing some fries. Next customer goes up to the counter and you can tell he's on something, speed or crack or something, he's talking loud and waving his arms like doesn't know he has any and she tells him they don't serve tacos here, try the place down the street with the big glowing taco sign, so he slams his fist down on the counter and it must've hurt but he'd never know and he tells her to get him a fucking taco and then decides he doesn't want to wait and puts his foot on the counter to launch over it and get his fucking taco and she screams in surprise or terror or something, I don't know.

I don't know.

Responsibility, liability, just a shot away, I don't know.

Gender relations, Summer Finn, reasonable fear, Kitty Genovese, I don't know.

Best foot forward, don't know, imminent injury, don't know, psychosocial, don't know, moral and political and economic and Dateline, and I don't know.

I can. I can. I can.

I can't move.

The manager runs over, shoves him off, steps out, and tackles him to the ground. She's there too, craning over the edge of the counter, bouncing on her heels, laughing, telling him to kick his ass, Eric.

There they all are, yelling, wrestling on the floor,

a painting on a wood wall,

a painting of,

kids on a playground in a park on a meadow of grass,

my god,

of the most perfect little blades of grass I've ever seen.

The Secret of Me
Nyla Alisia

    Were I to disrobe,

  would you see
    beyond
        ivory
            flesh,
take time to learn
    my
        secret
            language,
unravel the mystery
    of
        my
            sex,
discover Atlantis
    inside
        my
            silhouette,
decipher the enigma,
    clues
        whispered
in esoteric tongue,
    of
        simplicity
in the complex,
    the
        female
            of
                me,
under my skin,
    for
        you,
            undressed?

Taking Tragedy and Forgiveness to the Page
An Interview with Naseem Rakha

Naseem Rakha is the award-winning author of *The Crying Tree* (Broadway Books, July 2007), which was the recipient of the 2010 Pacific Northwest Booksellers Association (PNBA) award. The *Crying Tree* was also selected by BookExpo America's "Emerging Voice," Barnes and Noble's "Discover Great New Writers," and Target's "Breakout Writer" picks among others. Both an author and a journalist, Naseem's stories have been heard on National Public Radio's (NPR) *All Things Considered, Morning Edition, Marketplace Radio, Christian Science Monitor,* and *Living on Earth.*

Tell us a little about your background and your journey as a writer.

I was born in Chicago in 1959 to a Muslim Indian father and Catholic German mother. My father was an engineer, my mother was a homemaker, and we lived near the south side in an inter-racial middle class community called Lake Meadows. I was one of three semi-white children at Pershing School and, later, was one of many multi-racial kids at the University of Chicago's "Lab School." It was an exciting place and time to be a child: the Vietnam War, the civil rights movement, the environmental movement, and the women's movement were part of our everyday lives and conversations. Then a year after my family and I watched much of our surrounding neighborhood destroyed during the riots following the assassination of Reverend Martin Luther King, my parents moved my family to the safety (and the mind-utter blandness) of the suburbs.

Predominantly white, conservative, and Nixon-loving, I could not find a place among the kids who wore their bigotry like Boy Scout honor badges. My salvation? Louise Fitzhugh's novel, *Harriet the Spy,* the story of a young girl that finds her way in the world by noticing everything about it. Harriet was my hero: independent, determined, and undaunted by recrimination for being different. She wanted to be a writer, so I wanted to be a writer. Immediately, I picked up a pencil and began taking note of my world like a hawk eying a field for the slightest and most subtle movement and change. It was not a hobby, and not just "something to do." It became and remains the way I relate to my days, enabling me in the words of author Natalie Goldberg "to live twice."

I have come to think writers are created in utero. That, at some point in the fetus' development, the part of the brain which learns language and formulates meaning is supersaturated with whatever juice it needs for words to unlock the most exquisite emotions and compelling ideas.

But like many writers, my route to publication was not direct. My academic background was in geology, not English. It was not until I was 35, after traipsing the world as a teacher and consultant in sustainable resource management, that I applied for my first job as an official writer and I was hired by the Consortium for Public Radio to be their Salem Capitol Reporter.

I was a journalist for eight years. My stories won several awards and I covered a variety of subjects. I loved the work and the people I spent my time with, but I was getting tired of covering the same stories year-after-year, such as education funding, elections, strikes, etc. So in 2004, I took my first fiction writing class and I was smitten.

Could I have written *The Crying Tree* without all the detours? No. I likely would have never came up with the story if I had not been assigned to cover two executions in Oregon: one in 1996 and one the following year. On the less obvious side, the story is filled with the observations about land and people that I have made since I first read *Harriet the Spy*. I, unlike many young writers today, needed the life experience to flavor my writing. Journalism came in most helpful when it came time to do the leg work of writing. I knew how to research a topic, how to make cold calls, ask questions, and how to write under a deadline with multiple distractions. All this I learned in Oregon's Capitol press room but the rest I owe to Louise Fitzhugh.

Where did you get the idea for The Crying Tree?

On the night of September 8 1996, I stood on the grounds of the Oregon State Penitentiary watching as a group of rowdy drunks counted down the final seconds of a man's life. Inside the one-hundred-year-old walls of the prison, a man was about to be executed. He was to be the first man to die at the hands of the state in more than thirty years. The people popping beer cans and throwing firecrackers couldn't have been happier.

I was a reporter and I was ashamed. Not because of the revelers and not even because of what was happening at that moment inside the prison, but because I knew whatever story I wrote for the NPR would never convey the gravitas of that moment. I simply didn't have the elements for a good story. The condemned man would not take interviews and neither would the victim's family. All the journalists had were scripted statements from prison administrators and state attorneys and camera footage or descriptions of the props used during an execution: the room, the gurney, and the box of tissues waiting inside the witness booth.

It was not, I knew, enough to convey the importance of that moment, its emotional impact, and the reverberations it would set off in so many lives. One day I promised myself, I would tell the full story of crime, punishment, and the death penalty. It would be a story that looked at all points of view, the victims, the families, the attorneys, the condemned, and the men and women who must do the job of killing the condemned.

Following up on my promise, I sought out every opportunity I could to get myself into the state prisons. I interviewed inmates, staff, victims, and even men who had been exonerated from prisons. I also had the wonderful opportunity to interview Sister Helen Prejean, author of *Dead Man Walking*, for CCTV (the interview can be found on my Web site).

Then one day in 2003, I met a woman named Aba Gayle. She lived near me in Silverton and we began talking about the death penalty. She told me she had just came from visiting a "friend" on death row in San Quentin. When I inquired about this friend, I learned that the person was the man who killed her daughter. I was stunned. I did not understand how one could go from losing the most precious part of one's life, their child, to forgiving and even *befriending* the killer. Aba Gayle's journey was something I wanted to learn from and understand, so I began writing a novel, not based on Aba Gayle, but based on the painful and revelatory journey people are forced to take when faced with violent crime.

The Crying Tree is a character-driven novel. Where did your characters come from? Are they based on real people?

The birth of characters is one of the mysteries of writing. For me, it begins with my fingers gripping a pen and my mind in that ethereal space where memory and imagination begin to dance. For *The Crying Tree* I knew the main point of view character would be a mother and I knew they would live on a farm in Southern Illinois. I also knew they would move from their safe bucolic setting along the Mississippi River to the harsh, cold, and unprotected environment of Oregon's High Desert. Why? Because I knew both areas and the people who lived there and I knew the setting would mirror the emotional tension I was trying to create in the story. Beyond that, I only knew one other thing: the ending.

Getting to that end; however, was no easy waltz. Creating real, honest, empathetic characters was hard work. It required persistence, trust, and both halves of the brain working 24-hour days: the right side bundling characteristics and back story while the left side manages character traits like an artistic director. But, if I was not actively writing about my characters, then I thought about them, tested them, put them in different scenarios, saw how they reacted, what food they liked, what shoes they wore, what side of the bed they slept on and why. And if I was not actively thinking about them, I was passively ruminating, such as daydreaming in the shower, while driving, or making dinner. The characters in *The Crying Tree* were a product of trial and error and occasional hits of brilliance; those moments when something unexpected and revelatory was suddenly tapped out on the keyboard.

It is from those moments that people say characters "create themselves." But they don't really. Characters are the writer's children, born of our own sweet, and sometimes not-so-sweet dreams.

The Crying Tree explores some heavy themes like forgiveness, discrimination, and prejudice. What made you decide to tackle these topics and were they difficult to write? What advice would you have for other writers who want to explore similar themes and/or controversial subjects?

You are right, *The Crying Tree* does explore quite a number of "heavy themes," but that was not my goal. I knew the death penalty and forgiveness would be themes, but those have been handled in many books and in many different ways. What makes *The Crying Tree* different, I think, is that those themes are not the driving force of the novel. Instead, they are the natural and almost organic amalgamation of lives being led and conflicts being confronted. My goal, as I said earlier, was NOT to write a polemic. I think authors fail when they think, "I am going to write about global warming, or domestic violence, or discrimination, etc ..." The problem is if the theme takes over, then readers feel manipulated and even insulted. My goal was to show a real family with a real dilemma. The controversial subjects were just a natural consequence of living, not the dynamic in which I tried to pin a message.

Every novel has something to teach the writer. What do you think The Crying Tree *taught you about the craft of writing?*

I learned I had the focus, creativity, malleability, patience, and determination to write a book. If one of those things were missing, then I would not have written it. Writing a book is *hard* work. In a sense, writers act like puny gods as they create characters, their worlds, settings, lifestyles, belief systems, and conflicts that are not only believable but ring true to readers. This is essential. I am a very picky reader and will often get the urge to throw a book across the room if a writer sidesteps the critical task of really getting to know their characters. Shallow characters make for a shallow reading experience and I simply don't have enough time in my life to spend with superficial engagements.

I also learned that writers are, in essence, in a contract with readers. We are asking readers to give up a part of their lives to spend time with us and in our worlds. In exchange, we should give them something authentic; something that will make them think, feel, swoon, cry, and reframe their worldviews to include ideas they had not had before.

To do this, writers must have a strong sense of what they are working on and why. There are far too many naysayers out there willing and able to knock writers off track with superfluous questions such as: do you have an agent? Who buys books now anyway? And do you have any idea how hard it is to sell a book? I learned to walk away from those people and get back to work.

Tell us about The Crying Tree's *journey to publication.*

I had never attended a writing conference and had not given much thought to finding an agent other than occasionally looking at debut sales on Publishers Marketplace and keeping a list of the names of people who seemed to represent the type of book I was writing. Other than that, I just focused on writing day in and day out. Somewhere along the way I found out about Backspace, an online writers support group. I signed up for their newsletter, then promptly dumped each issue in the trash without ever opening the file.

Then one day as I sat in my favorite chair *trying* to edit what I thought was a pretty good version of my novel, I had an email from Backspace. I was reading, editing, trying to think, my son was poking some mechanical toy in my face asking me to fix it, and my husband was crying for help that he couldn't find the mayonnaise. So what did I do? I opened the mail from Backspace and found in big, bold, beautiful writing: AGENT AUTHOR SEMINAR NEW YORK CITY.

I read the announcement, looked at the manuscript on my lap, took the toy from my son; smacked it against my leg so that it started working again, picked up my computer, went in the kitchen, took the mayo from the refrigerator, handed it to my husband, and then pointed to my computer screen. "I am going to this," I told him. Then I went upstairs and took a shower.

I met my agent during Backspace's noon hour read-a-thon in New York City's Radison Hotel. This, I was told, was Backspace's alternative to the one-on-one meetings with agents that other writing conferences hold. At this highly masochistic event, a group of writers sat at a big round table with two agents. Each writer then read as much of the first two pages of their manuscript that they could get away with before an agent yelled, "Cut!" or "Stop please!" or "Yikes!" The agent would then tell the deflated writer why they would have dumped that particular manuscript in the trash. To say the process was brutal was an understatement, but it was also real, informative, and incredibly valuable for anyone wanting to know just what agents are looking for when they have a writers "baby" in front of them. It was also *very* subjective.

My first day I was told point blank: "Nice writing, but *no way*. It's too dark. No one wants to read about the death penalty." When I tried to explain that the book was really about redemption, I was told to be quiet. After all, I wouldn't be able to say anything if I had sent the work in.

I was crushed but I also learned a lesson. The agents I went to were looking for more "commercial" stuff than what I had produced. The rest of the afternoon I sat in the back of the conference room, not brooding, but researching. I googled each and every agent, reading anything I could about them. That was when I read that Scott Hoffman from Folio liked "dark" stuff.

I approached Scott as he was leaving and pitched my book. "Not for me," he said, "but tomorrow go to Laney Katz Becker. She loves that kind of thing." Needless to say, that was just what I did. I was the first person at her table and read my two pages. She then asked for fifty more and let's just say the conference was in November 2007 and I signed on with Folio the next month. For the next five months I worked with Laney to perfect the work. It was an awesome time. Then in May 2008 and after just 24 hours, I was offered a pre-empt from Random House. A week later, the book went to auction.

What would be your advice for writers hoping to get their work published?

Do write every day.
Don't say "one day."
Do read widely: Any genre, any topic.
Don't say "it's not for me."
Do mark up your books and write notes: What makes you laugh, what makes you cry, what makes you bored, what makes you aroused, and then figure out how the author did it. Don't read blindly, find the tricks and learn them.
Do find a group of people that you can share your writing with.
Don't listen to everything they say.
Do tell yourself this is important and then treat it that way.

Are there any new projects coming down the road?

I am deep into my second novel, which is another family drama, and looks at the issue of death and dying. This story is about a catastrophic stroke that forces a family to ask what is more kind: to save their mother's life or let her die. The story is set along the Oregon coast.

How do you think the Willamette Valley has influenced your writing?

I wrote much of *The Crying Tree* while sitting on my chair overlooking the Willamette Valley. It's a moody place with swaths of clouds coming in from the coast, curving around the hills, and blossoming out of ponds. I love moody weather. It suits me. I prefer weather that does not nag me to come out and play, or garden, or hike, or whatever I should be doing if I were not so neurotically committed to writing. I was the only person this past winter who was totally happy with the never-ending march of storms. It meant I could write without guilt. I like to write without guilt. It makes me very happy.

What do you think we can do to create a stronger writing community in the Willamette Valley?

I think writers could be doing more for kids. Let's face it, the schools are struggling (thank you very much Bill Sizemore and Don McIntire). We need to do all we can to put books into children's hands and teach them the magic of the written word. This means real writers in real classes, helping kids with reading, writing, editing, acting, and doing whatever it takes to grow that interest. I like the model the Seattle 7 have provided (www.seattle7writers.org).

What is your favorite thing to do (that you can only do in the Willamette Valley)?

Pick blackberries while I run and not worry about mosquitoes when I sleep under the stars.

Heather Cuthbertson
Editor-in-Chief

Sands of Oman
Naseem Rakha

I sit in perfect posture, legs tucked like Siddhartha under his banyan tree. But there is no tree for shade, no sweet girl bringing food or water. There is only sand, snakes, lizards, turbaned sheiks, and this sound—a transient note formed as the wind plies its fingers along the sculpted dunes. I have come to Oman to forget. Staring out—one whimsical wave of sand after another. Heat. Cold. Thirst. Hunger. Sacrifice beyond sacrifice. To face them and live, or not.

It does not matter.

War does this. It stalks me by day, sleeps with me at night, licks my breath in the morning and makes me want more. I hate it. I love it. Without it I would have been dead already, stuck some place – America most likely – numb as a wooden casket just waiting to be buried. I have reported on seven wars: Somalia, Kosovo, East Timor, Sri Lanka, Georgia, Rwanda, Afghanistan, Iraq. And still there are more. Lined up like tired travelers, queues of them on and on, shifting forever like the unflagging sand. Belfast or Belgrade, it does not matter—they are there: the generals and their soldiers, the war-lords and their insurgents, the penniless and pitiful.

It used to amaze me, the things I would see. Now, finding a human hand in a field is no more jarring then finding a drunk in a church, or a willow beside a pond. In fact, the willow would be more jarring. Is more jarring.

Sand.

It covers the dunes. Dozens of them climbing up out of the ground, hundreds, thousands, millions of dunes going on and on and on. And the heat exquisitely searing. My flesh perfectly scoured. Sand reaches into my clothes, my mouth, my stomach, my spleen. Its fine crystals glimmer in my shit. I bury the waste with more sand and move on.

The problem is one of metaphors.

I've run out. A machete's crack through a spine can sound like the whack through kudzu only once. And even then, the comparison does not suffice, for kudzu does not bend its pliant knees begging to be spared, it does not bleed. It does not scream. What metaphor is there for the cries of the child whose eyes are burnt from their sockets? Or, not even his cries, for cries readers know, they can imagine those. But what of the more specific sound of the hot poker penetrating soft flesh, and then the smell? What words will describe the posture of the people who are forced to watch? What does the umbilical-like grip of their fear feel like? And after it is gone, what follows? But of course, umbilical is a metaphor, and I shall use it—even if I already have.

After all, who cares?

More than likely, my stories are never read. Instead they are the text glanced over as you ride the train to work. Or drink coffee in a Starbucks. Or, the section of paper you fold neatly and place under your rain-soaked boots, or your puppy's rear end. For you are wise to know that you can never know. Even if you read, you can never know. Even in the places you've heard of—the Kabuls, the Darfurs, the Gazas. Or, the places you've been—the Harlems and Rio de Janeiros. You can never know. Just as I, as I watch the sand start to bury my feet, am hoping to forget.

The Housewife's Tale
Monica Storss

In mid-air, the snake is strangling the albatross.
I see this from my kitchen window while I put
Away the breakfast dishes. My husband has gone
To work for the both of us and I have gone to the garden
To watch the murder closer. The wind chimes are restless.
I am standing by the mint when the bloodlet drops
Scatter on my skirt and forehead.
The bodies fall twisting to the earth and the snake has won.
I lay my body on the ground by the apple tree
to watch while crouching. I open my mouth
and the snake slithers in.

I go back to the house, and wait for my husband to come home.

Shadows Of Evenfall
Nyla Alisia

In the Irish Countryside
F.I. Goldhaber

I followed the instructions,
as ludicrous as they seemed.
I parked alongside the road
across from the pasture gate.
A marker, no bigger than

a street sign, swayed in the breeze,
assuring me that I did
not trespass. I climbed over
the gate, walked through a double
row of trees. Just like she'd said,

it opened into a large
sheep pasture with dirty white
ovine forms scattered across
green hummocks and knolls. Turning
right, following directions,

I climbed the steepest hill. At
the top, I found my reward.
Only a small plaque explained
their significance. Standing
in a ring, as they had done

for millennia, I saw
a collection of boulders.
Some rounded, some flat, some tall,
no two alike, they formed an
ancient, Irish, stone circle.

Animal Souls
Brigitte R. C. Goetze

*In Memory of Waver Talking Dog,
also known as Will Rogers*

He never met a person he didn't like,
and though he'd snarl, when needed,
he never bit. What for?
A guileless heart
does not charge.

St. Catherine, medieval Solomon,
bestowed small souls to animals.
I'm no saint, but this I know:
only the blessed will love
so extravagantly.

Gray
Ariel

Salem thinks I exist in purple—
the multitude shades of it,
feminine soft lilac
bold, saucy plum
for I drape myself in them—
        but I don't …

I exist in the gray.

The middle ground, neither one or the other;
proud of not being pure but of being true.
Knowing in its different shades
I'm not lost in the dark,
not lost in unhealthy extremes.
Unlike newspaper, life is not black or white;
it is the two coexisting.
Note the early photographs—
how our past, our ancestors are exposed
in the mingle of light & dark,
their features, their angles, their shadows;
character defined within the grays.
There is despair there in the black,
stark severity in the white.
But in the gray is their dreams, their fears—
There is hope there.

So don't label me Republican
        Democrat
        Business
        Tree hugger
        Religious fanatic,
        Atheist

        Pro-Life
        Pro-choice.
Don't paint me with a broad brush,
don't paint me with color—
for it will not capture the truth.
To see me, take my photograph
distill it down to the abstract, to the concrete;
I will be exposed where they merge.
No man on the street.
No soundbyte of the day.
My gray silhouette is my own.

Life and Death and Flies
Heather Cuthbertson

When Mrs. Ashworth died, she fully expected to meet Apostle Peter at the pearly gates. Instead, she was directed to Fred. He stood behind a card table and wasn't much to look at.

"Ashworth, Ashworth, Ashworth," he said, thumbing through a stack of note cards. "Ah, here you are."

No book. No scroll. Just a single note card with a sticky note.

"Is that really it?" she asked.

"Budget cuts," Fred said. "Been like this ever since the baby boomers."

Mrs. Ashworth eyed the card in his fingers and wondered if it was still impolite to snatch things out of people's hands or if the little niceties and common courtesies changed after death.

Fred glanced at the card, looked up at her, then back down again, and finally nodded. "Not too bad, not too bad. Let me guess, you had a pretty normal childhood, went to college where you experimented with some drugs and maybe a girl or two. After you graduated, you got married, had a couple of kids, worked at a job you hated, and then taught Sunday School until you became one of the dearly departed. Is that correct?"

Mrs. Ashworth tightened her shawl. "Generally, I suppose."

He smiled. "Fabulous."

Mrs. Ashworth did not smile back.

"Now according to this," he said, flicking the card, "you have the choice of a bat, a hyena, or a baboon. Which will it be today?"

"Which will *what* be? Bat Heaven? Baboon Heaven? Hyena Heaven?"

"*As if*," Fred balked, "what kind of place do you think we're running here?"

"Well for a moment there ... oh never mind all that." Mrs. Ashworth chuckled. "Just Heaven, please. Bat Heaven, how silly."

"Right," Fred said, "because bats are reincarnation options and, lucky for you, it's on your list, along with baboons and hyenas. My name is Frederick, but my friends call me Fred, and I'm here to assist you in your reincarnation needs. You strike me as a lady who likes to push her weight around, may I suggest the baboon—"

"Reincarnation?" Mrs. Ashworth shook her head. "I don't want to be reincarnated."

"No offense, but …" Fred leaned forward and whispered, "you are in the reincarnation line."

"It must be a mistake. I'm supposed to go to Heaven."

"Have you ever been reincarnated before, Mrs. Ashworth?"

"I … I don't know. I don't think so."

"Then no mistake, you're in the right line. Each soul must complete an act of charity before entering the Kingdom of Heaven. I don't make the rules, it's just how it is."

"I've done plenty of charity work," she said. "I was a Sunday school teacher, which you already knew, and I volunteered at the local animal shelter every Saturday since I was 23. Not to mention, I was a board member on the Advocates for Literacy, Help for the Hungry, and Cancer Crisis Group. I hardly think I need to do any more charity, do you?"

"Sorry, no exceptions," Fred said. "Everyone has to go back. Even Oprah has to stand in this line."

Mrs. Ashworth glanced around her. "Is Oprah here?"

"No, but if she were, she'd be in this line, waiting for her turn like the lady behind you."

A woman hovered at a respectful distance. Mrs. Ashworth guessed they were roughly the same age (if anything, the other woman was older) and at their age and being dead and all, what was the rush?

Fred handed her a ballpoint pen. "Ready?" he asked.

She slowly took the pen, knowing deep down that something wasn't right. This wasn't what she had learned in the Bible. She was supposed to see her dead relatives, feast, and rejoice. Not go back as some filthy creature. This had to be a mistake. Any second now, Apostle Peter would put a stop to this and personally escort her to Heaven. Mrs. Ashworth just needed to stall for a short while; she really had no other alternative. Besides, Apostle Peter would want her to.

"What if I refuse?" she asked. "What if I decide not to do it?"

"Then you go into limbo until you do."

"What if the world ends by the time I decide, what then?"

"Cockroaches can survive anything."

"A cockroach? You would turn me into a revolting *cockroach*? Oh my … I think I'm getting faint." She pressed her gloved hand against her cheek. "Yes, I definitely think so. I best lie down for a spell."

"No problem, Mrs. Ashworth, but before you go I'm going to need you to circle your choice on the card and initial right above it."

"What if … what if I don't want to be one of those things," she said. "Maybe I would rather be a dolphin or a horse or a bird? Let me pick one of those and I could easily make my decision then."

"Not your choice."

"Then whose is it? Perhaps I could talk to them about it."

"God chooses and, trust me, I wouldn't question *His* judgment. I've seen it happen, not pretty."

Mrs. Ashworth gazed beyond him. "And this really is Heaven? You'd have to tell me if it wasn't, you know."

Fred scratched his chin. "That's a bit complicated."

"A-ha, I knew it." Mrs. Ashworth pointed her finger at him. "I knew this wasn't Heaven."

The growing line of people behind her began to murmur and turn to each other.

Fred glared at Mrs. Ashworth. "Way to go," he said and then held up his hands. "Calm down people. Calm down. Everything's fine. No need to be worried."

"Fibber," she said, crossing her arms. "You're a wolf in sheep's clothing. That's what you are. A wolf."

"Is that so?"

Fred snapped his fingers and the clouds parted behind him. The pearly gates shimmered as Mrs. Ashworth expected they would, the golden mansions glinted in the distance, and angels with harps floated in the air, singing "Oh come all ye faithful …" That was where she belonged, over there, in the distance, basking in holy light, not here with Fred, who was rudely blocking her view with his shaggy hair.

"I can tell what you're thinking with that gaga, gooey look on your face," he said, "but if you want to get over there, you have to take care of business here."

"And where's *here* exactly?"

"The Accounts Receivable and Transfer Station. But around the water cooler, we call it the Park and Fly." He laughed to himself. "Just a little apostle humor."

Mrs. Ashworth narrowed her eyes. "Amusing."

"Right." Fred coughed. "I suppose we've gotten a smidge off track and the line is getting long. I'm really not allowed to let it get 33 deep. Now about that choice ..."

The clouds melted back together, closing Heaven from her sight. Mrs. Ashworth could hear people grumbling in the line and telling her to get a move on. She couldn't stall much longer. Apostle Peter sure was taking his blessed time and, if he didn't get there soon, she would be scratching her backside somewhere on the Serengeti.

"Well?" Fred prompted.

"I ... I would like to formally appeal my reincarnation choices," she said.

"No, Mrs. Ashworth. No appeals process. No complaint forms. No skipping steps. Like I said, it's better just to get it over with. Besides, most return better by the experience. Enjoyed it even."

"I don't see how. Don't baboons throw their own feces?"

"Among other things."

"I don't see how flinging my ..." she lowered her voice "... flinging my feces around will make me a better person."

"Soul," he said. "You were already a person. And, don't forget, you do have two other choices."

"Hyenas are vile creatures and bats are plain filthy. Baboons are the lesser of the three evils in my mind, but not much better if you ask me."

"But Mrs. Ashworth ..." Fred shook his head. "... God loves all his creations."

"That doesn't mean I have to and you want to know what I think?"

"Not particularly."

"I don't think this is charity work. I think this is a punishment. You could at least have the decency of telling me what I did wrong, something I apparently had overlooked."

"It's charity work." Fred sighed. "Not a punishment."

"I doubt Mother Theresa had to do it."

"She was a jersey cow in North Dakota."

Mrs. Ashworth smirked. "I'm sure she found that lovely."

"Mother Theresa was a gentle soul who went back as a gentle creature."

Mrs. Ashworth was about to reply with something snarky, but she closed her mouth and placed her hand over her heart. She couldn't feel a heartbeat, but if she had, it would be beating a little slow because of her low blood pressure. Her lips started to twitch, then tremble. Her pink fingernails opened the purse she'd been buried with and fumbled for a tissue, which apparently some one had not deemed necessary to put inside.

Fred tapped the note card. "I really think we've spent far too much time on this and if you would only—"

"Is that how it works?" she asked, dabbing at her eyes with her knuckle. "You go back as the creature you were in life?"

He shrugged. "It's not an exact science or anything, but generally the loyal go back as dogs, the disloyal as cats, the weed smokers as sloths, and the artists as platypuses. It levels out one way or another."

"Was I so awful?" Mrs. Ashworth wailed, no longer caring if her mascara coated her cheeks in charcoal snail trails. "I tried to do the right thing. Honestly, I did. But in the end ... in the end I was a horrible person after all."

"What? I didn't mean that. Horrible? No. Come on, don't cry." Fred fiddled with his tunic and then a piece of his hair and then his ear. "What do I know really? I'm just the guy behind the table. Besides, you have three choices, not everyone gets three. Now that's saying something."

"A baboon, a hyena, or a *bat*. If that doesn't say wretched, then I don't know what does."

"They're not so bad. I'm a fan of baboons myself. And John, you know him, he went back as a bat once; said he loved it. I think Matt's gone hyena a few times. Would two of the coolest apostles I know go if they were wretched?"

"I suppose not." Mrs. Ashworth sniffed, starting to seriously doubt that Apostle Peter would show at all, but she couldn't give up, not yet.

"Then what about politicians," she asked, "what do they go back as?"

"Coyotes."

"Celebrities?"

"Parrots, macaws, and flamingos."

"Generals?"

"Lions."

"Garbage collectors?"

"Lobsters and raccoons."

"And Sunday school teachers fling *feces*?" she screeched.

"Really, Mrs. Ashworth." Fred sighed. "What more can I say? Charity and Heaven? Or limbo and cockroaches? Just please, *please* do me a favor and make up your mind before there's a stampede."

She had to admit the line was a tad long, nearly beyond sight. People died so much quicker than she expected and here they were, waiting to go back to the place they'd just left. After all her long years of depositing credits into her afterlife, Mrs. Ashworth felt gypped and holding out for Apostle Peter wasn't going to change things. He wasn't coming.

She dumped her purse on the table and clicked the pen. Fred pushed the note card in her direction and her hand hovered back and forth from choice to choice to choice. "I suppose," she said, "the sinners get the luxury of going straight to Hell."

"They go back as flies."

Mrs. Ashworth chose the hyena.

Ballet
Nicklas Roetto

Postcards from Iraq
Nicklas Roetto

0500 hrs.

Daylight pierces layers of black smoke with the sun's irritated iris. Let me see, the sun says. Let me see the dust draping the buildings like snow on Christmas morning. The wild dogs lapping pools of green algae. The red lights illuminating dirt on the helicopter pads. The broken palm trees, littering the charred desert. The mangled remains of trucks, homes, and children. Let me see, it says. Let me see.

0830 hrs.

A house sits, silent as a forgotten shrine, overlooking a plantation of grapes. Dust coats the adobe finish, seeping into the aging brick to its wooden bones. Colored rugs hang over the balcony next to a gray satellite dish. The dried veins of the vineyard rest on frames, long abandoned, long forgotten. A forest of trees, rumored to connect at the roots like fingers clinging to fingers, circles the plantation. A mother sits with legs crossed while her daughter runs through the tree trunks. Canopies of leaves protect them from the endless sand stinging their cheeks.

1000 hrs.

Five shadows darken the earth. The women pluck strawberries with hands stained the color of blood. Their charcoal dresses brush the vines like spiders edging along with slow purpose. A man with tired eyes stands in the middle of the field while the women circle him, orbiting like planets. They move away from him and each other, pulling against the threads of connection, thought, and intent. A woman stops to press her hands against the arch of her back. She gazes through the barbed wire fence as she has done several times before without a wave, nod, or smile to those beyond its perimeter, just a look to remind herself they're still there and she's still here in this small place of strawberries and blood.

1130 hrs.
Heat rises above the ground, rippling in waves of diesel exhaust. The orchards dance like muses among piles of copper wire. A soldier takes his lighter and burns a captured rat. "I like to hear them scream," he says against the background of guitar strings.

1200 hrs.
A mother and her daughter walk home, sheltering their faces with silk, from the market selling sandals and bananas. They pass the ruins of a village, staying close to its battered walls. The sound of tires shatters the quiet. Bullets rain down from above. Unseen within the shadows, a mother pulls her daughter against her; shielding her from things she shouldn't see and can't protect her from.

1300 hrs.
A boy skips rocks along the river. The water, as deep brown as his skin, courses to places he's never seen. He wipes his hands on frayed shorts and turns to his cow, grazing on scarce tufts of grass. He rubs a palm along its hide draped over its skeleton, exposing the crested arches of winged hips. He sits beside the animal, but never looks toward the base, lest he break his careful vigil. An Apache helicopter flies overhead. His mouth opens while he looks toward the heavens. There is something else in the world.

1330 hrs.
Shrapnel scars a radio communication station. Five men make their way outside to wash their hands and feet. Kneeling on ripped cardboard, they place their heads on the ground and face Mecca. Five times a day, their attention turns inward while armored vehicles taint the air with dirt and prayers travel on the hum of generators. Shalah.

1400 hrs.
Makeshift floors of plywood, polished by the flow of combat boots, lead from one tent to another like game trails in the mountains. Heart monitors and IV bags hang from hooked poles while medics stand over wounded combatants. A soldier rests between hospital sheets. Blood seeps from his amputated stumps. He resists the pain demanding to

overtake him and watches the door of the operating room for his comrade.

1600 hrs.
Vultures glide low, circling a crop field. Grains of sand take flight like dandelion seeds behind a mother's steps, traveling toward the gate. Folds of skin crease along her forehead; tears wash the dust from her cheekbones. She holds her daughter, limp in her arms, and presses her palms against the bullet holes, refusing to give the thirsty ground another sip. The blood seeps between her fingers, little by little, and dries on her knuckles. She pleads to her daughter, her voice pitching until her screams speak in the language of the thousands lost. The child's face grimaces with pain, but she has heard her. She has heard her.

2100 hrs.
A mother's eyes, black as raven feathers, talk for her; the track lines of tears whispers her story, and the young girl unconscious in her arms explains the risk of coming to the place of music, campfire, and jets half-mangled in the desert.

Will you take her? a mother asks a soldier.
Yes, he says.
Will she live?
I don't know.
Can I stay with her?
No. I'm sorry.
A soldier takes the child, leaving a mother alone and staggering on the isolated road.

2300 hrs.
Night curses the sand flies, but blesses the spiders and scorpions that scurry from the deep places of a crumbling mosque. A dim light hangs overhead as my thoughts guide my hand, writing the things I hold inside. They are my gift like that of the barley moon. "If I die, will you give these to her?" I ask.

Hotel Beloved
Tim Pfau

Hotel Nthatuoa-Beloved-waits on the spine
of Africa for travelers to January's
summer river washing the feet of the mountain who
spreads wings in gentle cover over beloved daughters.

Daughters faded from sight of eyes that saw and hold of
arms that held. Whether from the dust of corn and cattle
or the rains of Oregon, our beloved daughters gone.

Where travelers rest and heal, worn travelers you would
expect to find in Qacha's Nek, Lesotho where you
did not expect to travel, so why would they? Lovers,
foreign volunteers, and village girls with jobs in town.

Beloved daughters on their own, lonely and proud now.
Risen to working with bank's crisp paper or teaching
while listening to passing cattle's low moans outside.

Red bricked, one rose bush, Hotel Nthatuoa, Beloved,
named for a daughter who died, an ending you were steeled
to accept before you came, before you even learned
she lived, even though you knew all sons and daughters die.

But not your own beloved daughter, a volunteer,
taller now, asleep beyond, with her tan limbs tangled
in love and regret, pride and youth's determination.

Hotel Nthatuoa's night holds you between sheets, or
purging your traveler's flu into her white porcelain bowl,
hearing the rural songs, roosters in call and response
on erotic dreams. Dogs, surely yellow, chanting Bass.

Then comes a quiet time while your own beloved
spouse finally sleeps, slowly breathing healing mountain air,
in Nthatuoa's soft embrace, cool next to your own.

Listen to the silence of Lesotho's summer dawn.
No urban sounds disturb the clear far chimes and laughter
lifting you gently, quiet, to wash in beloved
Africa's morning greeting to you, uprooted man.

Look across the river. Lift your eyes to the gold line
just cracking darkened mountain's arching edge. Listen to
the slow fall of beloved goat's bells and herdsmen's calls
flow down the unseen rocks to meet the loving water.

In the Room There is a Painting
Marc Janssen

In the room there is a painting
 A picture
Protected by glass
 Shiny bright
Next to the picture window
 A soul
That reflects the images of cars
 Rushed moving
In a blue winter dawn
 A morning
They slip between the frames
 Cold lost
Headlights glancing
 Never seeing

Talking Verse with a Novelist
An Interview with Lisa Schroeder

Lisa Schroeder is the author of the Young Adult novel *I Heart You, You Haunt Me* (Simon Pulse, 2008), which was a 2009 American Libary Association (ALA) Quick Pick for Reluctant Readers and a 2010 International Readering Association (IRA) Young Adults' Choice Selection. She's since written three more novels in verse for Young Adults and two Middle Grade novels including *It's Raining Cupcakes* and *Sprinkles and Secrets* (September 2011), both from Aladdin Paperbacks.

Which is easier for you to write, a conventional novel or novel in verse? Why?

Each one has its challenges. For some reason, writing in verse comes easily to me. I'm not sure if it's because I started out writing picture books and really love the challenge of telling a story in as few words as possible or why it is exactly. I've sort of stopped trying to figure out why and I just go with it. But certainly it's not always easy trying to write something that is poetic and accessible and tells a story all at the same time.

Whatever I'm writing, story is always number one. It has to be. The format that story is told in should never get in the way of the story. And so, some stories are going to come more easily than others, regardless of how they're told. The things that cause me trouble are the things that cause all writers trouble at times —developing characters, figuring out tricky plot points, etc.

What made you decide to write in verse form? Had you seen it done before? Was it a difficult sell?

Before I wrote my own, I had read the Newbery award-winner *Out of the Dust* by Karen Hesse and all of Sonya Sones' books (I am a huge fan). It never occurred to me to try writing in verse myself. I had a dream one night and woke up and went to the computer because I wanted to get the story down that was in my head, which was about a girl whose boyfriend had died, but he loved her so much, he didn't want to leave her. When I started writing, it wanted to come out in this sparse, poetic way. It really scared me. I didn't know if I had the skill to do a whole novel in verse! But the book poured out of me and whenever doubt would creep in, I told myself to finish it because I wanted to know what happened.

It was definitely a hard sell. I'd done something that not many authors had done. I'd taken what was traditionally a literary format and combined it with more of a commercial idea. Fortunately, I found an agent who loved it and thought the verse gave it an atmosphere I couldn't have found with regular prose. We got 9-10 rejections before an editor at Simon Pulse read it and fell in love with it. Pulse is great about publishing things that might be a little bit different. They don't shy away from things–all they want is a good story they think teens will connect to.

I'm pretty sure the book surpassed everyone's expectations. It went into a second printing just one month after its release. Today almost four years later, it's still on shelves and still selling, now in its tenth printing. I call it "the little book that could."

How are you so productive? You've had 6 novels published in 4 years with 2 novels released this year alone. Were any of them in the works for a long time? Did you write them at the same time, switching back and forth?

Yeah, I write fast. Please, dear readers, don't hate me. I'm able to write at least two novels a year, and last year I actually wrote three. My verse novels are shorter, and if I get into a story and it's going well, I can write a draft quickly. The hard part is then going back through to work on word choice and the poetic elements and all of that.

I always work on one draft at a time. But the nice thing about writing middle-grade and young adult is when I finish a YA novel, it's freeing to switch to middle grade and do something different. Middle-grade is actually where I started. I wrote three middle-grade novels that weren't good enough to be published before I sort of fell into young adult. Writing *It's Raining Cupcakes* and the companion, *Sprinkles and Secrets*, were just so much fun to write. I was a huge reader when I was in that eight-to-twelve-year-old range and, as an avid little baker, I would have eaten these books up (forgive the pun). I wrote *It's Raining Cupcakes* at a time when I needed to write a book like that. My second YA novel, *Far From You*, came out at a horrible time when the U.S. was dropping into a recession and people were being laid off right and left. It didn't do nearly as well as my first novel, and I felt so disappointed. And everywhere I turned, there was bad news, it seemed.

I decided I needed to write a happy book, a book that would make me smile and others as well. I literally brainstormed things that make people happy and, somehow, my brain landed on cupcakes. I thought, "Wouldn't it be fun to write a book set in or around a cupcake shop?"

Back to your question, there really isn't any secret. Write every day. Use the time wisely. Don't let the negative voices get in the way. Whenever I start to worry about this or that, I tell myself to finish the story because I want to find out what happens. It's really important, even more so now, perhaps, that I block all of the business junk out of my mind when I'm writing and just get lost in the story. I write for myself first and foremost. I try to have as much fun while I'm writing as I can. It's not always easy–writing can be really hard work. The days when the words flow like water? There's nothing like it. You have to put in the time in order to get there though.

Were there any drastic changes to one of your novels during the revision process that readers would be surprised to hear about?

After I got the editorial letter for *Sprinkles and Secrets,* I knew I had to basically start over. A lot of things needed to go and new scenes added in their place. So I sat down, opened a blank document, and started typing. The first five chapters were almost entirely new. I was then able to do some cutting and pasting from the old document every now and then. But a lot of the book was rewritten during that revision process. And the book was so much better for it. I think that's one thing I've really learned over the years–it's important not to get too attached to our work. We have to be able to let things go and trust that we'll be able to come up with scenes that are even better.

I Heart You, You Haunt Me *came from a dream. How long from the dream until the book deal?*

I wrote the book in March and April. I got feedback and revised over the next six months or so. I landed my agent in November and we sold the book the following March. So about one year from when I started writing it to when we sold it.

What's the next project in the publishing works? Middle-grade, picture book, YA, novel in verse, none of the above?

I've recently sold my first fantasy middle-grade to Henry Holt, but I don't have a publication date or even a title yet. They are hoping to find an illustrator to make the book really special, so I suspect that will take some time.

I also sold a YA novel this year, my first one not in verse, and that one is scheduled to come out in Spring, 2013. We're working on the title, so again, nothing I can share yet. I will update my web site as I have new information to share though.

What's your advice to writers of every age about the publishing arena, whether how to enter it or how to survive it?

I heard Markus Zusak speak years ago and his advice really resonated in me. He said, "Don't be afraid to fail." To me it means, don't be afraid to try new things, to explore lots of possibilities, and see where they take you. I could have stopped writing on page 10 of *I Heart You, You Haunt Me* because I was afraid of failing. I really had no idea if I could pull off a whole novel written in verse. It would have been so easy to quit and say, "I can't do it," but I kept going. I've learned that each book teaches us something, and it's never a waste of time to keep writing, even if it might not ever sell. I think of my unpublished novels as my schooling.

The advice is good for those seeking to find an agent or editor as well. Don't be afraid to fail. Send the query out in batches, and if they're all rejected then you know something isn't working, so you revise and try again. This business is hard, and you really need a good deal of tenacity to make it.

When were you able to quit the day job?

I worked 32 hours a week at Oregon Health & Science University up until January 2010 when I quit. A number of things led me to the decision, none of which were that I was making a ton of money as an author and could afford it. It was just getting harder and harder to juggle everything, and the day job was getting really demanding. I was actually so scared we wouldn't make it financially. But we had a savings account in place, so my husband and I decided to give myself six months of writing full-time to see what might happen. I wrote

The Day Before shortly after I quit and we sold it in April. And then I wrote *Sprinkles and Secrets*, which we sold in September. Once I had a couple of sales, I was able to relax. I really hope I'm able to continue doing this for a living. It's hard work, but I love being more available to my family and being my own boss.

How many of your novels are set in Oregon?

The Day Before is my latest YA novel and it takes place in Newport. Many favorite attractions are in the book, such as the Yaquina Bay Lighthouse, the aquarium, Mo's Restaurant, and others. One local reader said, *"The Day Before is almost a little love letter to these favorite places."* For this book, I wanted the beach experience to be as authentic as possible, so I purposefully set it in a place where I could easily go and do research. I wrote the first draft from memory, but when it came time for revisions, the whole family went down there and we spent a weekend visiting most of the places the main characters, Amber and Cade, visit.

It's Raining Cupcakes and *Sprinkles and Secrets* are both set in Oregon, but I made up a town for those books and called it Willow. When I did a book signing in McMinnville, one of the girls asked me if I'd modeled Willow after McMinnville, because she thought the towns sounded similar–a small, friendly town where kids felt safe riding their bikes places and that kind of thing. I was like, wow, maybe I should move to McMinnville!

Obviously, I know Oregon best since I was born and raised here, and I think it's a pretty special place. With each book, it takes some time figuring out the best place to set the story. It's always very intentional, and I really hope Oregonians who read *The Day Before* like those personal connections they'll have with the story.

Marilyn Ebbs
Executive Editor

Reading Lillie
Jean Rover

The day Lillie and her friend, Bunny, caught the Greyhound bus in the Burger King parking lot, they told their parents they were going to a movie. Once the bus roared off toward Portland, Lillie opened her vinyl purse and pulled out a tube of cherry lipstick, which she carefully applied using a tiny mirror. She clipped plastic white earrings shaped like giant lifesavers to her lobes.

"What are you doing?" asked Bunny. "I thought you weren't allowed to wear lipstick."

"I don't want the psychic to think I'm just some country hick. Besides, I'm thirteen now."

Lillie ran a comb through her brown hair and pulled it back into a ponytail to resemble the style of a movie star she'd seen on the cover of a magazine. There wasn't much she could do about the zits on her chin, her flat chest or the dark-rimmed glasses that rested on her nose.

Bunny had a chunky figure and two prominent front teeth, which earned her the nickname. "Where did you get those earrings? They look dorky."

"I got them off Mom's dresser. As soon as I can, I'm going to get my ears pierced."

"You're such a dreamer," Bunny said.

Lillie and Bunny had been friends since the first grade. Bunny was good at playing the piano; Lillie sang in the youth choir, which she considered training for Broadway. It dumbfounded her that Bunny only wanted to entertain her mother's church friends.

Lillie said, "All the actresses have pierced ears."

"You've never been in a play," Bunny snickered. "Don't you think you should start soon?"

Bunny's words stung. Lillie had tried to audition for a lead role in the class play, but the drama coach made her a stagehand. "Lillie, you're so dependable," he said, checking his clipboard.

"I … came to … try … to try …" The words stuck in her throat. She didn't trust herself to say more. He didn't even notice her. Maybe she should get a tattoo.

The bus chugged into the transit mall. They walked fifteen blocks to a dingy, brick apartment building and made their way down a dim hallway. There was no sign on the door, so Lillie knocked. A dark-complected man peeked out. She hadn't expected a man.

He growled. "What do you want?"

Lillie held out the small newspaper ad. "We're here to see the psychic."

"Is that all?" He had a gold earring in his right ear and huge teeth.

Lillie nodded.

He turned away and they followed him inside. "Have a seat." He motioned toward a small sofa. His eyes roamed from Lillie's red lips to Bunny's ample body. He stared at her budding breasts. He smirked, then disappeared behind two heavy gold curtains.

Bunny said, "That guy is weird. What if there is no psychic? What if he's a serial killer? No one knows we're here."

"Shhhh," said Lillie. "He might hear you."

Bunny sniffed the air. "It smells like sweaty gym socks in here, kind of skunky."

"I think it's some kind of sage. Psychics always burn incense."

They could hear the man talking with a woman.

"Two young girls ... kids," the man said. "They just want a reading."

"No stuff?" the woman asked.

"Just a reading," he said.

"You sure?" she asked. "No stuff?"

"Didn't I just say they were kids? *Nunca escuche.*"

"*Ay dios mio!*" she said. "Give me a few minutes. I'll get ready."

The girls heard shuffling behind the curtains. Bunny said, "This place is creepy."

"Jeez Bunny, get over it. Psychics need to be a little weird. That's what makes them psychic." Lillie tried to sound confident, but her stomach felt like it did when she sat in the dentist's chair.

The man came out from behind the curtain. "Madam A will see you now."

Bunny looked at Lillie. "Madam A?" She giggled.

Lillie nudged her, and they followed him through the curtains into a room lit by candles.

Madam A, a dark, heavyset woman in a low-cut blouse, sat at a round table covered with a gold damask cloth. A huge crystal ball gleamed from the table's center. "How can I help you?" she asked. She wore her black hair pulled straight back from her face.

"I want a reading," said Lillie. "This is my friend, Bunny." Bunny smiled.

"You got fifty dollars?" Madam A asked.

The small ad never mentioned the fee. Lillie opened her purse and pulled out an envelope. She had emptied the jar from her underwear drawer. It was money she had earned picking berries for new school clothes. "I only have twenty-five."

"Fifty dollars," Madam A said again.

"Couldn't you do it for twenty-five? We came all this way," Lillie pleaded.

Madam A's small eyes darted from Lillie to Bunny, then back to Lillie. "Okay, I'll do it for twenty-five. You sit over there," she motioned to Bunny, who moved to a chair in the far corner. Madam A stuffed the cash in her brassiere. Then she pulled out a pink cigarette lighter and lit a candle on the table. She looked at Lillie's left palm with a magnifying glass and traced the lines in it with one finger. "Hmmm," she said as she worked. "Close your eyes and concentrate very hard. We must tune our minds to that which is above."

After a few minutes, she ordered Lillie to open her eyes. When she did, it seemed like a little waft of smoke came from the crystal ball, which suddenly brightened.

Madame A asked, "What would you like to know?"

"I want to know my future. When I'm grown up. I want to be an actress, or a singer, a famous ice skater, or a dancer, maybe. Will I? Who will I marry? I don't want to marry a farmer. I want to live in Paris or London. I don't want to can pears." The words tumbled from Lillie lips. She gripped the side of the table like a defendant waiting for a jury verdict.

"Whoa," said Madam A. "That's a lot for twenty-five dollars."

"I don't want to be like them ..."

"Like who?" asked Madam A.

"The women back home. Nothing happens there. They get fat ... never go anywhere. They work in the cannery in the summer and their hands are rough."

"Come closer." Madam A smelled like cigarettes. She removed Lillie's dark-rimmed glasses and pulled off the elastic clip holding her ponytail. She pulled a tissue from her bosom and wiped Lillie's lips.

"Ah," she smiled. "Much better. Do you know the story of the ugly duckling?"

"You mean the fairy tale?"

"Whatever. One day you will turn into a majestic white swan."

"Will I be an actress, a famous actress ..."

"A swan, you will swim many places."

"But an actress?"

The psychic looked into the ball again. "I see a swan swimming."

"What about an ice skater or …"

"Is there an ice rink in that tiny town of yours?" Madam A sounded irritated. Lillie thought she heard Bunny's stomach growl.

"No, but …"

"I see a swan swimming in water. There is no ice."

"A singer then? Please." Lillie moved to the edge of her chair.

Madam A pursed her lips, leaned forward and looked directly into Lillie's eyes.

"You have pretty gray eyes. One day you will blossom, fill out, become a lovely, young lady." Lillie lifted her face. She felt like a flower opening to sunshine on a spring day. She had never thought of her eyes as anything but ordinary. And did she say lovely?

"Many things will happen." Madam A looked into her globe. "I am seeing a swan, a pretty swan. Oh wait, she's swimming with a handsome dark swan."

"Marriage!" squealed Bunny.

"Shhhhhh," Madam A hissed. "Not another word; you'll break the spell."

"Where am I swimming?" Just then, a bell rang. It sounded like the timer on her mother's oven.

"The ball is getting cloudy, the spirit is leaving," said the psychic.

"But …" Lillie said.

"Just keep doing what you are doing," said Madam A. "You will find the way."

"Which way?"

The psychic stood. "I can tell you no more."

The man came back into the room.

"Show these young ladies out," Madam A said. She threw up her hands. "*Tengo tanto que hacer.*"

Lillie and Bunny followed him to the door.

When they reached the street, Bunny said, "It must be over ninety degrees out here."

Lillie didn't notice the August heat, the tall buildings, or all the people on the sidewalk, rushing somewhere. Her eyes sparkled and her face was radiant. No one had ever told her she was pretty. She stuffed her glasses into her small purse. Her fingers gripped the elastic clip she had used to pull her hair into a ponytail. She tossed it into the street.

Maybe she didn't need a tattoo.

No Man's Land
Lois Rosen

Boy was I in for a shock. Never in a million years did I expect to find myself in a no man's land called Oregon. My daughter Harriet and her big ideas - she couldn't find a fine university in New York? She wants to study art, not that I'm saying she isn't talented. But I didn't break my neck working extra shifts at Weiner's Bakery so she could study four years in a second-rate college, then starve in a garret. And if painting it absolutely has to be, you tell me where else could she find more galleries, museums and schools than in Manhattan? She could have saved me a bundle living at home, commuting on the Express Bus and shoot downtown in what? A half hour, forty minutes, tops.

No, she has to go and get herself a scholarship to study at some podunk school, Willamette University. Who's ever heard of it? Before I left here last week to fly way the hell—pardon my French—across the country to visit her for Parents' Weekend, which I couldn't have even afforded if my sister Bitsy didn't give me her frequent flier miles, Harriet and I talked on the phone, for maybe five minutes. The calls cost a fortune. She says, "Mom, I told you before, you're saying it wrong. It's not Will-uh-met, it's Will-am-it."

"Okay, all right. Will-am-it. You're happy now?"

She says, "Mom, I'm not trying to hurt your feelings. I'm just wanting to help you, so people here will get what you're saying. And it's not Or-a-gone, it's Or-i-gin."

"Please. I've lived all my life in New York, where we act like civilized people. If my pronunciation isn't good enough for the cowboys you want to spend your life with at a school that has—what did you tell me—thirty-two Jews out of four hundred something, I can cancel my flight right now."

Freedom Walk
Samuel Hall

Cradling the bolt-action Weatherby in the crook of his arm, my Zulu guide, Elijah, pointed to the dry earth. A rhino's footprint stared up at the hot sun, daring us to find its maker. The track was minutes—perhaps only seconds—old. Crushed blades of grass slowly lifted from the pulverized oval. I imagined the tremendous force that could instantly transform matter from three dimensions to two. Far off, the cry of a bird pierced the silence of Mkuzi Wildlife Reserve.

Elijah did a complete three-sixty, his eyes searching the tangle of trees and bush that surrounded us. Then he turned to me. "You must climb a tree, any tree, if we see the rhino. Do not wait, not for a second." I nodded and tried to swallow. I hadn't planned on a black rhino. Those beasts weigh up to 4,500 pounds, and can move 50 meters—165 feet—in three seconds. That was about the distance to the nearest tree, a sweet thorn festooned with menacing spikes.

I hardly knew Elijah but I could tell he was alarmed by the sight of that footprint. Not a pleasant surprise on this sullen morning but here we were and that massive animal was somewhere very close. Now fear became my reality, taking form in the shadows of every thicket. Not mere anxiety, but the possibility of abandonment and total vulnerability. Elijah would avoid hippo and croc territory and supposedly knew the location of the elephant herd, but one doesn't go strolling about when a black rhino is in the neighborhood. Never mind that Elijah held the only weapon between us. If we encountered that lethal package of destruction, I'd have to take care of myself.

I'd been excited at the prospect of seeing animals in their natural habitat, because of the challenge but there was something else. From my youth onward, I had wanted to walk among wild animals just as Adam did in the biblical account. Like others, I took risks to see if I could assert control over forces that might do me in. That drew me to work in Africa—the setting for the most primitive forces in nature.

I began to envision ways to escape or avoid a charging rhino. Climbing or dodging behind a tree would be my first move—if I saw it in time. Failing that, Elijah could hopefully divert its attention. As a last resort, he had the Weatherby. Indeed. Those options were dependent on a host of factors, all chancy.

Since Elijah was mainly concerned about the rhino, I would be, too. No need to dwell on other creeping and crawling possibilities as long as I could avoid getting separated from him. I didn't let myself think about trying to find my way back alone to the fenced compound where my family waited for my return.

My temples felt as if electrodes crackled inside my head. The act of breathing, a suddenly complicated affair, dried my throat. I slowed to listen. No sound but the muffled rush of the long grass against our legs, and the occasional birdcall, announcing our route. I'd heard there was something life-affirming in coming close to death. Perhaps I was about to find out.

At that moment, I had the novel idea to pray. God was the Familiar One in that primeval place. I felt ashamed that only then had I thought to call on God. But I began to pray—quite fervently, in fact. Walking through that tangle of trees and scrub, I silently asked that my imaginings would not become my reality. Words from the Psalms came to mind, proclaiming God as a rock and refuge ... as a strong tower. A sense of peace returned. How could I have forgotten? Of course, God was there.

Just then, Elijah crouched and pointed beyond a small clearing. A lordly kudu bull grazed only 40 meters away, jerking his head up frequently to test the air. A vagrant breeze brushed my face. Slowly, I raised my 35 mm Olympus and framed the antelope in the viewfinder, his spiral horns glinting in the sun. In the silence, the click of the shutter seemed magnified. The kudu flung his head up again. His razor sharp senses caught scent or sound, and in an instant, he bolted and was gone.

That majestic animal had stood before us for a full minute. In the exhilaration of seeing him, I'd forgotten about the rhino, but not for long. The thoughts came as if it had been there all along and all it needed was my awareness of reality to manifest itself. Anxiety asserted itself the way a jackal materializes out of a matrix of grass and sickle bush. I wanted to be gone from there, yet I didn't want to leave. The tantalizing thought that I could remain in control beckoned and as quickly as I'd thought to pray, I abruptly forgot about God.

The intermittent cry of a bird became my fixation; it was nothing less than a bugle call of our location to unseen ears and eyes. I knew that red-billed oxpeckers always accompanied rhinos, cleaning their hides of ticks. Was that chittering the sound of an oxpecker?

I watched Elijah, trying to discern his thoughts. He seemed oblivious to lurking danger. Fine for him, he had the Weatherby. Besides, being a Zulu, his sharpened instincts could probably detect the presence of animals—hadn't he seen the kudu first? I wondered if he would stand his ground if a two-ton rhino rumbled out of the foliage.

An explosion of movement and grunts erupted on our left. My heart in my throat, I tried to find the source of the commotion. Not knowing which way to jump, I remained rooted where I stood. Two grotesque heads rose like dragons out of the earth, confirming the implanted image of a rhinoceros. By the time I comprehended what I was seeing, two wart hogs had dashed away, tails raised like radio antennae.

In their wake, a cloud of dust coated the underbrush, reassuming the blanket of silence over the bushveld. I started breathing again and Elijah gave a nervous laugh. He'd been scared, or at least startled. Knowing that actually made me feel better. We turned back toward camp, opposite from where the wart hogs had fled.

That walking safari was more than just a heart-stopping experience to add to my journal. My desire to go there—compulsion, perhaps—seemed to come from a yearning for an undefiled place, a place that had always existed within me. My experience wasn't unique. Such a craving or nostalgia for a primordial paradise is found in the writings of ancient civilizations that sought to commune with God or those they called gods in a place without fear of creatures or of one another.

From fourth century B.C. China, Taoists told of an ancient age when the nature of the people was what it ought to be.[1] The Greek poet Hesiod (eighth century B.C.) wrote that during the Golden Age, people lived among the gods and freely mingled among them.[2] The ancient Hebrews accepted the creation account in the Bible about the Garden of Eden.[3] Other references can be found from tribal cultures from Africa and India to the Americas and Australia. Those traditions were preserved as the records of actual historical times and places, not as myth.

I consider that my experience derived from a memory of Eden, the place of no fear. Regardless of one's belief, there seems to be a universal longing for that which was, and which is found closest in nature. Blaise Pascal called this human restlessness "a God-shaped vacuum in the heart of every man which cannot be filled by any created thing, but only by God, the Creator, and made known through Jesus."

When I saw that rhino track, my walkabout was a gift I didn't want to accept. But my quest for Eden could only be experienced by working through my fear if I could. As I emerged from that primeval wood, I felt empowered and competent, even jubilant. It was a single step in my journey to freedom and self-discovery.

A gazelle flashed across our path as we returned to the compound. It happened so quickly that I blinked to assure myself I'd actually seen it. Only minutes before, the cry of the unseen bird had pierced the air—not insistently, but more as a benediction to the morning. Amazing that such a clear sound from nature could quicken the human soul.

---

1. Sacred books of China, Part I - Translated by James Legge (1891).
2. Hesiod: Theogony, Works and Days, Shield. Translated by A. N. Athanassakis (1983).
3. Genesis 2-3; Psalm 104; Isaiah 11:6-9; 40:28-31; 45:18; Ezekiel 28:13; Romans 8:19-21.

Vertigo
Melanie Patterson

Panis Angelicus
Michael M. Pacheco

Mochi was a mestizo, part Aztec Indian, part Mexican. He stood at the door of the one-room hut he shared with his mother and father, leaned on the doorframe, and gazed south. His homeland was still there, hundreds of miles away.

Over the span of a decade, the majority of his tribe in the Yucatan Peninsula had migrated to America, seeking a better life. He had come with his parents, along with others of their tribe, to this land. This Nuevo Mexico felt empty, so different from the old one.

People had left the Yucatan in droves. The so-called beautiful North had devoured his neighbors and strangely, they were never heard from again. For reasons unknown to him, his family never made it past this part of the country, the Chihuahua Desert, a hot and desolate wasteland.

The economy here wasn't much better than the one they'd left behind. If he could, Mochi would join his father and work the fields. However, at his tender age of thirteen his mother thought it best that he obtain an education while the opportunity was still there. She enrolled him in the local church school with the white nuns in black dresses.

Mochi promised her he'd do his best, yet it pained him tremendously to see his parents struggle to put food on the table.

"I wish I could make things better," he said to Sister Mary. He confided in her and felt comfortable around her as she was only five years older than him.

"Have faith, Mochi," she'd say in her velvety voice. "Things improve when you focus not on the shadows, but on the bright side."

When Sister Mary looked at him, her eyes embraced him. He wondered whether she had that effect on everyone, that feeling of instant intimacy. An emerald green, giving off the appealing gleam of precious stones, they flattered him the moment they fell on him. The directness of her gaze made him feel as if she was interested only in him.

With Sister Mary's help at school, Mochi improved his Spanish and learned some words in Latin, instead of the language of his parents and ancestors. He learned math and writing, and he tolerated the religious teachings about Heaven and Hell, God and Satan. But without question, what he relished was learning to read and perform music.

Sister Mary taught him to play the violin, an instrument which he'd never seen before. In six months, he was playing as well as her, and she was amazed at his progress. She said he should be at a conservatory, not the mission.

Mochi possessed an unusual sense of timing so precise that he didn't use a metronome any more. He practiced in the morning before going to catechism and then again at night before going to bed. He pressed down on the strings so much that his fingertips bled before they blistered.

"Oh, mijo," his proud mother would say. "You're amazing and you play music fit for heaven."

But what was a violin virtuoso to do in the desert? He was lost in a barren sea of sand with only a small village to his south and nothing but more sand and craggy rocks to the north.

The first notion of a problem arose when Mochi was late on his way to an evening event at the church. The sun had already set and dusk was quickly becoming night.

The itinerary called for a lecture about faith, then Mochi and Sister Mary would perform. The violin duet featured Mochi and he was very excited. Word had spread beyond his village and people from nearby communities would be there to see and hear his performance.

Father Aquinas was to talk about faith in the Book of Hebrews. Mochi had memorized it. "Faith is the assured expectation of things hoped for, the evident demonstration of realities though not beheld."

Mochi didn't know who the Hebrews were, not exactly. He had a vague idea they were like his people, a tribe that had traveled across great distances in the desert of their country. He wondered whether the Hebrews had fared any better to improve their lives than his family.

All that talk about Hebrews, divinities, and holy ghosts baffled Mochi. It wasn't that he didn't know about gods. It was just his were different. The gods he grew up with lived in the trees and on the sacred mountains. Each tribe, and there were many -Aztecs, Tzotzil, Tzeltal, Lacandon, Tojolabalis and Mayas- possessed its own pantheon of spirits. There were good and evil gods and even capricious ones that you could bribe with sacrifices and charms.

Mochi thought of these things as he was leaving his home. Lobo, the family pet, began barking in Mochi's direction.

"Quiet boy!" yelled Mochi over his shoulder. "There's nothing there."

As the words left his mouth, Mochi stepped on a stone and lost his balance.

He fell forward onto his knees, and then his side. He would have crushed his violin into pieces had he not brought it close to his chest to protect it. As he started to rise, something bit his right Achilles tendon. Mochi saw a rattlesnake, shorter than the length of his violin.

"You little devil," he said. He picked up the harmless-looking viper with his bow and flicked it away from his path. He stood and the world spun for a brief spell. When he regained his orientation, he continued walking.

He began walking and traveled what seemed like a mile when he heard music. It was a hypnotic melody, different than any he'd rehearsed. He listened and wondered whether he was imagining this beautiful sound. It lifted him and then let him down gently. He was an eagle soaring, a horse galloping with reckless abandon. He was in tune with the soothing melody, the dizzying crescendos, and even the staccato choir in the shadows. He could not cry though the joyous tears within were ready to burst.

What was it that made him feel this way?

It was God himself, no doubt, speaking to him, putting Mochi at peace. He knew Sister Mary and the others were waiting for him, but for a few minutes, they didn't matter.

Then a voice spoke to him. "Beautiful music, isn't it?"

"I love it!" he answered. Then he caught himself, realizing he was talking to no one. He spun around. The full moon covered the desert landscape in a blue blanket with cactus and bushes along his path.

He was alone. He knew that. Yet, someone had just spoken to him as clearly and softly as Sister Mary. He knew that he was being watched. A cool breeze ruffled his coal black hair. He stopped moving, cradling the body of the violin, hand on the bow to strike out if necessary. He worked a bit of spittle down his throat.

A bush a few yards away began to glow softly, pulsating nature of the red and yellow fiery light, flinging cactus shadows on the ground.

Then the voice spoke again. "Don't be afraid, Mochi. I won't harm you."

Mochi was intrigued not only by the glow coming from the burning bush, but also by the fact that the fire did not seem to destroy the plant whatsoever.

"Who are you and what do you want?"

"I am what you've been looking for, Mochi. I will make your dreams come true," answered the glow.

Mochi was dumbfounded. How did this entity know his name? How in Heaven did it know anything about him?

"The music you hear," the bush said, "it's like food for the soul. I can grant you the ability to play like that."

Something wasn't right. Mochi felt it in his feet. It was a numbness that reminded him of walking with his father on the snow-capped mountains in his homeland. There, his feet had gotten so frigid they seemed to not exist anymore. That same sensation was now creeping up his legs. But he hardly cared at all, as long as he could go on hearing that music.

He did love the music.

Mochi boasted, "I can already play well."

"Yes, but I can also make you wealthy. You do want to help take care of your family, don't you? You can even help the tribe rebuild your village. You won't need the silly church anymore."

Mochi thought about Sister Mary. He liked her. In fact, maybe he liked her a little too much, and fantasized about taking her as a wife. He skipped a day of catechism after he caught himself staring at her when she bent over. Something about the contours of her hips stirred things inside him.

And it was true. He wasn't fond of all the rote memory and the supplications that went on and on. He was a good – no, great – violin player, but to be better still. That was beyond his wildest dreams.

The voice asked, "Do you want to taste the music?"

"What?" asked Mochi. Then, without any voluntary movement on Mochi's part, his mouth opened wide. Musical notes rose from the glow like fire-lit butterflies fluttering down his throat. The sensation was pure ecstasy.

In his delight, Mochi forgot about the church event. He saw himself and his family back in the Yucatan. He briefly thought about his mother and wondered if she'd be angry with him. Not if she knew the peace he felt right here, right now. He closed his eyes and took it all in.

When the music stopped, Mochi saw the glow fade. He wasn't ready to let the feeling go.

"Wait!" he yelled. "I want to play music like that. I'll do what you ask."

Then out of the corner of his left eye Mochi caught some movement. He turned and saw the disembodied head of Sister Mary on the ground.

"Dear Jesus." His body shook in fright and he felt like he might urinate.

The blood-dripping head of Sister Mary spoke to him. "You mustn't go with him, Mochi. You'll be fine on your own. Have faith."

"No," screamed the bush so loudly the shriek hurt Mochi's ears. "You have tasted my spirit and you are mine forever!"

Sister Mary's disembodied head dripped blood from the corners of her mouth and her eye sockets.

Mochi considered only two entities that could make a disembodied head speak, God or the Devil.

When Mochi failed to appear at the church, they launched a manhunt. A cloud cover settled over the village and blackened the moon. The villagers searched and searched in the night but did not find Mochi.

They found Mochi's rigid body the next morning a mile north of his home, lying with his mouth open, clutching his violin.

No one ever knew how Mochi ended up walking into the desert wilderness instead of toward the church. But it is said that on the darkest nights of the year, you can walk into the desert, close your eyes, and hear the sad melody of a violin playing music fit for angels.

Reflection
Danny Earl Simmons

If I were not afraid

of becoming white, wind-scraped bones
in the dry of a thorny dead ravine
long after hovering and foul feeding;
if I were not afraid

of one turned back after another,
an end to coffeehouse debates,
and never seeing another eye squarely;
if I were not afraid

of shaking hands with her Galahad
every other weekend too soon after the red
fades from her eyes and my stinging cheek;
if I were not afraid

of a bent caney man
looking this way then that
for someone to tend his grave;
if I were not afraid,

I would succumb until golden
passion meets breathless exhaustion –

then break all my mirrors.

A Wagging Tale About Wagging Tails
G.R. Vince Johnson

After doing some research, I have concluded that steak would be a little less expensive if cattle didn't wag their tails so often. While observing a feedlot recently, I counted how often cattle wag their tails. Some tails only wag 8 times a minute and some as much as 12. It, therefore, seems logical to assume that on average, cattle wag their tails about 10 times a minute. Further observation revealed that the tip of the tail swings on an arc of about 8 feet and an average tail is about 3 feet long. To average things out I used 1.5 feet per wag and found it's logical to assume the entire tail wags about 6 feet per wag.

My calculations are amazing: Each critter wags its tail about 60 feet per minute. This comes to 3,600 feet per hour or 43,200 feet per 12-hour day. Egad. This comes to 8.2 miles per day. I will admit that my methods are a little loose; nevertheless, it is obvious that cattle expend a lot of energy in tail wagging.

I'd guess cattle tails weigh about 12 pounds. This means ten wags a minute amounts to 120 pounds of tail per minute, or 7,200 pounds an hour. Holy Cow. This means they wag 86,400 pounds of tail every 12 hours. That's 43.2 tons a day. Incredible.

My numbers on pounds and miles of tail wagging ignore the fact that cattle hold their tails straight for brief periods. This would seem to take a heap of force, but it would take all day to determine how often this actually occurs, so I decided to limit my findings strictly to tail wagging and forget the other stuff.

After making this tail-wagging discovery, I sat and pondered. My little pickup truck weighs about 1.5 tons. Cattle wag the weight of nearly 22 of my pickups a distance of 8.2 miles in a 12-hour day. Wagging all that tail, all that distance certainly requires a lot of vigor.

Think about hogs for a minute. You never see hogs wagging their tails. Their tails only weigh about 8 ounces, so even if they wagged them thirty times a minute, the amount of oomph required would not be as significant. This could explain why it takes less feed to make a pound of pork than it does to make a pound of beef.

I think it's time cattlemen went to some topnotch genetic engineers and asked them to come up with bob-tailed cattle. The way I see it, all that energy used to wag 43 tons of tail 8.2 miles every day would be better spent being converted into beef rather than fly swatting. If cattle didn't waste so much energy wagging their tails, I could have steak once or twice a month rather than just two or three times a year.

The Voice of the Turtle is Heard in Our Land
Bob Gersztyn

Guests filed into the room, people as varied as John Fahey's complex life: musicians, record company executives, artists, professors, and street people. John, the founding father of the steel-stringed acoustic guitar and considered the Guitar Players' Guitar Player, influenced many modern day musicians including Thurston Moore of *Sonic Youth*, Pete Townshend of *The Who*, and Chris Funk of the *Decemberists*. His style of playing was as eclectic as his personality, assimilating every style he came in contact with, from early blue grass and country to blues, jazz, classical, and eventually industrial noise. And on stage, he didn't just pluck strings. He could stop mid-song, go to the bathroom, come back 10 minutes later, and pick up right at the note he left off. And the only reason he ever lost an audience was because of his refusal to perform. Despite his worldwide fame, John spent his last years in Salem Oregon barely hovering above homelessness and in poor health until succumbing to heart failure complications in 2001.

I sat among a hundred mourners that February afternoon inside the Willamette University Law Library as the air slowly thickened with the scent of perfume, laundry detergent, and body odor. For someone known for his music, it seemed fitting that what brought John and me together was an album cover. Only then, it was a photograph of John standing in front of the half-demolished Senator Hotel, an image I had taken four years ago that captured the beginning of our friendship.

Back then, I was a freelance stringer music journalist for *Guitar Player* magazine along with half a dozen other music publications, but did photographic work on the side. Tim Knight, John's booking manager, asked me to do a photo shoot for John's new band, "The John Fahey Trio." It was the first time I met John and I wasn't sure what to expect. I had a somewhat jaded view of rock stars, having been exposed to a number of them through music journalism assignments. Even though I had read about John in the newspapers and music magazines, I wasn't familiar with him as a musician. I had only heard his most recent album, City of Refuge, which was hailed by everyone from *Rolling Stone* to *Entertainment Weekly* as the comeback album of the year. I thought it was a somewhat strange mix of alternate guitar tunings and industrial noise, since it didn't include the intricate finger picking technique that made him famous.

It was mid-July and I made it to Guitar Castle, our designated meeting place in downtown Salem. The guitar store was already locked by the time I got there. I stood outside, watching the heat radiate off the surface of Court Street at 5:00 PM. Across the street, a late-model Toyota sputtered to a halt, sending a cloud of sulfur dioxide in the air. A bear-like man emerged from the driver's side and bounded toward me with a youthful grace and exuberance that took me by surprise.

He reached out to take my sweaty hand. "I'm John. Are you the photographer?" His voice had a hint of whimsical humor.

"Yeah," I said. "Tim told me that you wanted to do some shots in front of the Senator Hotel."

John nodded. "It fits the kind of experimental industrial noise we're playing. Where are the other guys in the band? We were supposed to do the shoot together."

"I don't know," I said. "The shop was already closed when I arrived. Looks like we're the only ones here. That's okay. I wanted to get some shots of you by yourself anyway. Let's head over and get those done while we wait."

We walked over to the ruins of the Senator Hotel. Augmented by the oppressive heat, the acrid smell of pulverized brick, concrete, and plaster seeped into my palate. With the distant sound of rush hour traffic droning in my ears, we walked around the partially leveled Senator Hotel. In 1928, the hotel was one of the largest in town and flaunted its luxuries, but now it looked like something from the aftermath of Hiroshima.

After finding the best angle, I shot a couple dozen images of John until the heat got to us and we decided to call it quits since the remainder of John's crew were still nowhere to be seen.

John wiped his forehead. "Wanna get some ice cream?"

"Sure," I answered, thinking about where we could go. "How about Baskin-Robbins in the Salem Center Mall? It's air conditioned."

"Nah. I don't want to deal with a lot of people."

"Okay, there's a Dairy Queen close by."

"Let's head there."

As I drove toward the bridge into West Salem, John pointed to a group of homeless guys near the Union Gospel Mission. "Those are some buddies of mine," he said. He had met them when he stayed at the shelter. He had also lived out of his car. John had royalties coming in, but he said, "I'm on an allowance. If I had too much money in my pocket, I'd just spend it on prostitutes."

We ordered large vanilla ice cream cones, which John reluctantly allowed me to pay for. While it melted and dribbled down our fingers, we talked about the Union Gospel Mission, the way it was run, and the politics of religion used over the homeless. Usually when I met a rock star they were polite and friendly, but I really didn't have that much in common with them, since I wasn't a musician. When I would try to find a point of common interest, it seemed forced rather than natural and the conversation would usually fall flat. With John it was different. It was like having a conversation with somebody that you just met on the bus without any ulterior motives other than passing the time on the ride.

Over the next month, I photographed John with the other group members on the streets of Salem and performing at Berbatti's Pan in Portland. By the time that I brought the proofs to John, we had discovered a deep mutual interest in religion.

John had a degree in Religion and Philosophy from the American University in Washington D.C. and I had a degree in the Bible and Theology from a Bible college in Los Angeles. I was starting to write about the religious aspects of music when John told me that he thought and wrote about religion constantly. I mentioned to John that I had become a Protestant Pentecostal minister after being raised a Roman Catholic and he began to throw out insulting remarks, trying to get my goat. Instead, I asked him for an interview.

We met at the Oregon Capital Inn, which didn't have air conditioning included in the weekly rate. I entered John's room filled with at least 100 vinyl records, stacked on the floor and on the bed. He pointed to the lone chair. "Have a seat. Be one second."

John went into the bathroom with a 42 oz. plastic cup from a convenience store. I went over to the chair. There were some wet towels in front of it. I moved them to the side and smelled my palms. They reeked of sweat and body odor. As soon as John left the bathroom, I went in to wash my hands. When I got back, John was sitting on the bed with his cup.

I turned on the cassette recorder. "We're recording."

John rustled through a pile of papers inside a cardboard box. "I don't have a copy of it."

"Don't have a copy of what?" I asked.

"My paper where I attack the Protestant church as being Neo-Gnostics."

"Sounds interesting." I rocked back in my chair and looked at the peeling green paint on the ceiling.

"I don't have a copy of it though. I don't think. Do I?"

"You think the Protestant Church is Gnostic?"

"Neo-Gnostic." John said. "I don't know how serious I was, but I really let them have it while I wrote it anyway."

John inserted a straw into the plastic cup. He sucked up a mouthful of water, spat it out into his hand, and then poured it on his balding head. The water ran down his face and neck and onto a towel on his knees. I remembered the pile of wet towels I had moved earlier and the smell I had to wash from my hands.

John finished with the ritual and said, "The Roman Catholic Church was founded to baptize people and serve Eucharist. If you took away the Eucharist, then there wouldn't be any reason for it to exist, right?"

"Eucharist is the sacrament that purifies the soul," I said. "The believer eats the body and blood of Jesus Christ and becomes Him. The Eucharist is the—"

"Culmination of the Christian life," John interrupted.

"Yeah but it's mostly a symbolic practice."

"No. No. No. No. You're talking about Protestants. Catholics think they are eating and drinking His blood."

"Okay so you're into transubstantiation; the wafer and the wine actually becoming the body and blood."

John shifted in his seat. "Now we're just talking about an intellectual thing here, let's not get personal."

"I'm not. I haven't gotten upset with anyone over religion, except maybe when I was a brand new Jesus Freak."

John dumped the soaked towel on the ground and grabbed a new one. "What was the question again?"

"I was asking about the difference you see between the Roman Catholic Church and the Protestant Church."

"Sacraments and knowledge."

After that interview and several more following the next couple of years, I submitted our recorded conversations to a couple of publications. Eventually, an online folk music magazine published one of the interviews.

I sat through the funeral, listening to George Winston play John's composition "Steamboat Gwine 'Round De Bend" on the mouth harp. My thoughts drifted back to that hot summer day in 1997 when I took John's photograph standing in front of the Senator Hotel.

I didn't meet John until the twilight years of his life, but his creative energy still manifested itself through a variety of art forms: painting, writing, music, and religious investigation. I only knew John for four years, but in that short time I felt privileged to be included in his inner circle even if for brief moments. A year after John's funeral, I placed a pair of sunglasses on his gravestone just above the words "THE VOICE OF THE TURTLE IS HEARD IN OUR LAND" and took a picture.

Hand Colored Image of John Fahey in Front of the Senator Hotel Ruins, circa 1997

Bob Gersztyn

Working for the State
Ariel

Keeping job requires
new skills today-balancing
the State on her back.

Sold
Darren Howard

Soren never would have seen the ad if the dentist hadn't made him wait so long. At the time, of course, the wait was killing him. He called his crew to make sure they were on track to start painting the next house in a day or two. He called his wife to let her know he might not be able to pick up their daughter from school.

It was an hour past his appointment and the receptionist wouldn't meet his eye. Every magazine in the room was a women's magazine—how to lose weight, manage your hair, have better sex, juggle career and family, that sort of thing. He flipped through one and a single sheet of glossy black paper fell out.

He picked it up and was struck by the design. A network of lacy white lines shimmered across the page, subtly shaded to suggest depth on multiple levels. In each corner of the sheet a white hand, stylized almost beyond the point of recognition as a hand, pointed to a white oval with a question mark centered in its face. The hands resembled both penises and guns.

The banner asked, "Why? How? When will it happen for you?" Below that, a toll-free phone number. That was the whole ad.

He looked up at the receptionist. No sign of life.

He dialed. Four rings drilled into his ears and he almost hung up. The fifth ring was severed with a click and a sound like wind.

"Hello?" he said.

"Yes. Yes. Hello indeed." The deep grainy voice of an old man.

"I saw your ad—I think it's an ad. You hooked me. What are you selling? Viagra?"

A slow chuckle came through the phone. "You know. You know ... Hmmm." The man positively purred as he trailed off.

Soren's smile disappeared. He shifted in the chair, uncrossed his legs, and leaned his elbows forward to rest on his thighs. "I have an idea. So?"

The rustle of wind downshifted, as if the man on the other end had turned against it. "You're calling from Oregon, I see. The other Salem, is it? There is a hat in the park outside City Hall. The edge of the fountain. You can leave a deposit, earnest money under the hat. Let's say a hundred. Hmmm."

The wind cut off.

The hygienist opened the door. "Mr. Soren, so sorry for the wait."

He couldn't move for a moment as he tried to figure out what had just happened. The hygienist beckoned impatiently and he followed her in for his appointment.

After the hygienist poked and scraped him for half an hour, the dentist took one look and told him he had a mouth full of cavities, as usual. He'd need another appointment to have them filled. The receptionist smiled as she handed him the reminder for his next appointment. "See you soon, Mr. Soren."

He went back for the ad, but the magazines were now fanned out across the end table, showing just a corner each, and the sheet wasn't anywhere among them.

"Was there a loose page here? A glossy black ad?" he asked the receptionist. She smiled and shrugged. "Not that I saw."

On his way back to the job site he almost didn't go to the park, but then he told himself it would be stupid not to go, as if he were scared. It wasn't out of the way; he'd just make sure there wasn't a hat on the fountain and leave.

As soon as he saw the fountain, he became less jaunty. A grey fedora lay perched on the corner of the basin. Soren looked around to see if someone was setting him up, watching from behind a tree.

He sat next to the hat and half expected it to move away as someone jerked on a hidden string. It didn't move. Two men in suits walked by, deep in conversation. When they had passed he lifted the brim of the hat cautiously. There was nothing underneath, and he turned it over to look inside. A slip of paper was tucked into the ragged felt around the inner rim.

In neat, handwritten script, it read: *Congratulations, your time has come.* Underneath, the penis-gun symbol pointed to an oval with a question mark.

His heart thudded as he reached for his wallet, pulled out five twenties, and slipped them under the ribbon of felt. On his way out of the park he looked back at the hat and didn't see anyone moving toward it.

As he got in his car he got teary, suddenly overwhelmed with an odd mixture of joy and guilt. He didn't want anyone to find out about this new bill he was paying, but he was glad to pay it.

Months passed, and years. His daughters grew up. One married. The other went to college and came back each summer with a new boy. His business swelled in the boom that came after the recession. Once his daughters were out of the house, he and his wife began to look each other in the eye and smile more often.

But every once in a while, whenever things began to weigh on him, distract him from his surroundings, his phone rang with a number that displayed all zeroes. Only wind on the other end. He snuck away to the park, left money under the hat, and walked away, lighthearted again.

One day he answered the phone and instead of wind, heard the old man's grainy voice. "Soren. Are you ready? Hmmm."

Before he left, Soren took a look around the house and kissed his wife on her forehead, and then again at the nape of her neck as she turned away. Outside, the sun was brilliant and he began to whistle, glad to know he was to be rid at last of the humdrum complexity, delivered from the shame of his secret expense.

Arrows
Monica Storss

i've made candles from your clementines and open-sky spaces
filled with arrows
filled with cowboys who can't sit still
the range is still open
and lapping against the packet boat like tiny newfoundland waters:
small, quiet:
except in january.

i would meet you at noon, underneath the obelisk for three straight years
if i weren't splayed akimbo elsewhere, reconciling.
the apples will drop rotting from the tree.

you flashy and chauvinist,
you opal and queer,
but wait! you've shot the doe
six times this sunday
making my mouth
which has never touched death
(well, only once: father)
quiver.

To Know Too Much
Frank Yates

This town, I hate. Reminds me of East Berlin before the fall. Nothing but concrete, dirt, smog –"Watch where you're going, jerko." I hear – ugly people.

Get a grip Boris, it's your last job. Woolen collar around my neck, I pull – last time. No overcoats in Peru. Key in hand – my ticket to freedom. No more contracts, congested cities, crowded airports. Soon, it's Casa Boris in jungle with wife yet to find.

Fighting the gusts; steps, I climb. Post office drawer down the hall. Door opens; note, I see with map to bank, new key, and identity. Who's my employer? Another CIA target? Someone who knows too much? Too many secrets, glad it's my final kill.

To the bank, I walk. No cab drivers to recall a face. No trolley commuters to hear a voice. Bank clerk greets me. Throat, I point; "laryngitis," I mouth. Lid, I open – another key, map, photo, account transfer confirmation. My final pact for death. New passport, Lima bound – red-eye tonight.

Next stop, Greyhound depot. Locker, gym bag inside. Men's room; new clothes, old in trash. As building inspector, I walk.

Chain links surround demolition site. No trespassers allowed, city employees only. Lock keyed. Stairs climbed. Lookout found. Rolex checked – half-hour to kill.

I wait. Demanding career – longer than most, they say.

I wait. Notches are many – no way to brag.

I wait. No wife, no family, no friends – delayed until Peru.

I wait. Why this man? Why this place? Why me?

Hour arrives. Cartridge loaded. Scope sighted. Out opening, I peer. No mark in sight.

A flash. I jerk. Shoulder explodes where my head should be.

I drop. A bullet whistles by.

I know too much. The target is me.

Noteworthy Event
Kathleen Saviers

Earl imagined the deliveries he made contained treasures or news of lost loves. Significant events. Such things never happened to him, but today, Earl would have such an experience.

999997.6

Earl had driven the same delivery truck for more than two decades and the odometer was about to reach one million miles. He laughed off the ribbing he took from his co-workers who thought the epic moment trivial. Even his wife didn't appreciate the significance of his truck's noteworthy event. She thought it was silly.

He sped towards the Johansen place for more than one reason: the odometer and Melody. Melody must have bought and sold on one of those online auction sites because as many packages went into her house as went out. Earl glanced at the odometer.

999998.7

Melody was a petite woman with flaming red hair and the nicest legs he ever saw. She was fancier than his wife, Sally. Even her name was fancy. *Melody Johansen.* It rolled off his tongue and over his lips. "Sally" was a stay-at-home wife, afraid of computers.

Earl pulled into Melody's driveway. He would make the delivery; pick up her newest packages, and right when he was pulling out, it would happen. One million miles. Reaching the milestone right after Melody's house made it even more extraordinary. He had his camera ready on the dashboard.

999999.2

Less than a mile to go.

His feet danced toward the back of the truck. He pulled the packages out and headed toward the front door where Melody was always waiting for him with her movie star smile. Except this time, she wasn't there.

Earl frowned. *Strange.*

He pushed the doorbell and heard loud chimes from inside the house. He listened for the click clack of Melody's feet. He peered through the stained glass window and saw boxes in the entryway. He rang the doorbell again and waited. Again and waited. Once more and waited. She wasn't coming.

Part of Earl wanted to go, but another part of him wouldn't let him. What if something was wrong? What if she needed help? He couldn't leave without knowing she was okay. He cupped his hands around his eyes, pressed his nose against the window, and looked past the boxes in the entryway. Two of the nicest legs he ever saw lay sprawled on the tiled floor.

Bang. He hit the door with his meaty fist. Melody didn't move. Bang. The glass panels shook in its casings. Bang. Bang. Bang.

"Melody ... err ... Mrs. Johansen! Are you okay?"

Earl turned the knob. The door opened. He hesitated on the threshold. What was the company policy about entering a client's house? Was there a policy?

"Mrs. Johansen. It's Earl. I'm coming in. I just want to see if you're okay? Are you okay? Do you need me to call an ambulance or anything?"

Usually when Melody stood in the open doorway, Earl smelled roses. Now the house smelled like Gregor's Butcher Shop. The soles of his shoes squeaked like a thousand mice. "C'mon, Mrs. Johansen quit fooling around."

Earl stepped around the corner. His eyes watered and he felt his feet pushing him back to the door. Melody's robe hung half open, revealing little blue flowers printed on her pajamas with matching fuzzy slippers on her feet. But a scarlet puddle of blood surrounded Melody's beautiful face in a rippled halo.

Holy Mother of God.

The oatmeal and bitter coffee he had for breakfast came up his throat. He wanted to make her beautiful again. Make her purple face pink. He stared at her, searching for a way, but nothing was coming to him. There was no amount of first-aid that would make her lips smile.

He ran. He didn't mean to. He just did. When he got outside, he remembered the cell phone in his truck. Somehow he stammered out the address to the emergency dispatcher. He leaned against his truck to keep from falling, saying her name over and over again. *Melody Johansen. Melody Johansen.*

A deputy stepped out of a patrol car behind Earl's truck. Earl hadn't heard him pull up.

Earl pointed to the house. "There's a dead woman in there."

The deputy approached the house. All Earl could think to do was wait in his truck. He tried to picture Melody as she was before. Sexy legs. Foxy smile. Movie star hair. That was how he wanted to remember her, but all he could see was her bloated face, purple, bruised, and her eyes void.

The front door slammed. Earl jerked in his seat. His hands fumbled for the keys in a semi-daze. Melody was going back inside. He had delivered the packages.

He glanced over and saw a deputy carrying a large clipboard. It hadn't been a dream. Earl stepped out of the truck.

The deputy sighed. "How are you feeling?"

"I don't rightly know." Something about all this wasn't right. He felt bad, right down to the bottom of his gut. Like he'd lost something really important, something he didn't even know he had. He didn't even feel this way when his parents passed away or when his sister died in a car accident.

The deputy asked the rote questions: name, address, where he worked, and why he was here. "We need to notify her next-of-kin. Do you know if she's married?"

Earl nodded. "Yeah, but I've never seen him. I think her husband owned some kind of a business."

"What about kids?"

"No, I don't think she was the mother type."

"Why would you say that?"

Earl shrugged. "She looked more like a movie star or a model and she dressed too nice to have kids puking on her. The house looked neat too. At least from what I could see."

"Are you going to be okay?" The deputy asked.

"Yes ... no ... I don't know."

"Do you need to sit down?"

"Yeah, probably. This whole thing has been a shock." Earl sat on the curb. The concrete ridges cut into his pants. "Was she ... was she murdered?"

The deputy tucked the clipboard under his arms. "That's for the medical examiner to determine, but it looks like to me she fell and hit her head. Nice floor, but slippery as hell."

Guilt washed over Earl. "What if ... I mean, if I had been here sooner?"

Could I have saved Melody?

"She's been dead a few hours, probably before your shift started."

Earl wiped his forehead with the back of his hand. "She was nice." He nodded his head and stared across the street at a patch of wildflowers, getting slowly strangled by some weeds. The flowers looked sort of like the ones on Melody's pajamas. "She was a nice lady. Something special. You know?"

The deputy cleared his throat. "Yeah, well, thank you for notifying us. Here's my card. Give me a call at the end of the week. I might have some more information then."

Earl's hands trembled as he took the card. And that was it. He would never see

Melody's smile again, never admire her legs, and never smell roses at her door. She was a lost treasure, a delicate item smashed in the box. He got into his truck and crossed her name off his delivery list.

He couldn't finish his route. He turned back for the warehouse. He wanted to hug his wife. Tell Sally he loved her. Earl's fingers opened and closed on the steering wheel. The light in the intersection turned red and a car swung out in front of him. He jammed on the brakes to avoid a rear-end collision. When the truck stopped, just in time, Earl covered his face and let out a lungful of air. First Melody and now this. A horn honked behind him. The light was green. Earl seized the steering wheel and looked at the dashboard.

000004.7

Displaced
Nyla Alisia

- My toes sink in and sweet-grass makes room. A prairie flower may be plucked from this place but her roots cannot be torn from the red soil. (My journal, Cheyenne, Wyoming - July 17, 1993)

The prairie

so far away,

closing eyes,

I am there still.

Warm wind

makes love to skin.

Thunderheads roll

the horizon

like ghost-dust

remembering buffalo.

Summer washes sky

barely blue,

more bleached

than bones.

Wading deep,

sweet-grass waves

tickle legs.

White poppies

intoxicate

bumble bees

large as pony beads,

wings drumming hard.

I was born

already buried

in this place,

womb of thought

brings rebirth,

delivers me

to red-soil earth.

Lingering palpable,

a heartbeat

heard even now,

it's melody

calling me back.

I am

bound there still,

veins running wildness,

I feel it

inside,

the mustang

pounding in my chest.

Kalends of September
Stephen Eichner

18 Elul, 3828
Kalends of September, 68 CE

Remember the Sabbath day and keep it holy. Six days you shall labor and do all your work, but on the seventh day is a Sabbath day of the LORD your God: you shall not do any work—you, your son or daughter, your male or female slave, or your cattle, or the stranger who is in your settlements. Exodus 20:7

What evil thing is this that you are doing, profaning the Sabbath day! This is just what your ancestors did, and for it God brought all this misfortune on this city! Nehemiah 13:17

It was inevitable that, soon after I began writing my *t'shuvah*, I would feel compelled to restore Jewish structure to our precarious lives here. When his regime fell, Nero took most of his entourage down with him. I am exceptional to have survived this long. Do my enemies in Rome still hunt for me, or am I forgotten?

I anticipate this confessional with only partial relief, as if testing my legs after confinement in sickbed. I am resolute in beginning strict daily observance to counterbalance the radical changes taking place, both in Rome and within me.

To those born and raised in a close Jewish community, as I was in Antioch, the ancient customs cling like our own skins. A few were destined to shed those skins and transform into new beings, adapted to prosper in the outside world. This I did for many years. However, as my *t'shuvah* progresses, I realize that these were lost years, swollen with appetites for wealth and sensuality, pursued with impunity.

Before taking refuge here, I set aside orthodoxy while enjoying riches, lavish diversions, and an Emperor's protection. I equated fulfillment with the empty busyness of commerce. I now realize delusion and hypocrisy defined my actions. I believed my Shabbat wine operation would appease the ruling class while somehow facilitating the coming of Mashioch. Even while immersing myself in vulgar city life, savoring multifarious palace entertainments, I believed that I was God's instrument through which his will would prevail. It did indeed: but violently, spared no one. Nero's hubris has been overthrown; I am in hiding, terrible reprisals are sweeping the lands—and still no Mashioch.

As I write, I begin to recall what Reb Yigal taught me many years ago: Mashioch will come at a time of cataclysm, only when the rich and powerful have devoured one another, and only when the righteous have proved deserving. I will do my part by readying myself through close observance of the law, and my *t'shuvah*. The High Holy Days are nearly here, and atonement is due. I am overcome by dread. I fear that I may further offend my God, and that it is too late to set matters right.

We live secret lives in an obscure rustic villa. We have ample reserves and an army of coloni vine-workers, who were once German tribal warriors. With such advantages we may yet survive these civil wars.

Though I resolve to make life here one of strict observance, I find I am still frustrated by estate business. As the Days of Awe loom, our grape harvest has begun. The vines sag low and the moon-signs are favorable. Weeks ago I had my Roman agent, Patrolicus, order a new drive shaft and wheel-stones for my main wine press. Delivery is overdue.

Not long ago I would have worked the pagan coloni through Shabbat to install the new equipment so the wine crush could begin without costly delay. When the equipment arrives, I will need to make a decision. The workers await my direction.

It has been quiet since Atticus Ruffina's regiment terrorized my household that early August morning. My servants are languishing and aimless. The sound of passing travelers on the road sends them rushing into the garden where they bob and peer furtively through the cypress branches. They mutter to their amulets of Udjat as they watch the passing cavalcade. Increasing military and post traffic traverse the roads these days, while the numbers of civilians dwindle. Merchants, once my colleagues, now hurry past, threadbare and frightened, mute testimony to the spreading anarchy across Italy. So far no one has given this house a second glance.

I am aware that my servants are uncomfortable with my compulsive writing and inattention. The heat compounds their idleness and apprehension. All three, particularly Arsinoë, have turned superstitious and regress into Egyptian necromancy to relieve the tedium while I am absorbed in work. I have found dead house spiders under my bedcovers, mummified in bundles of dried grass and unraveled thread. Yesterday I found another votive offering in the corner of my bedroom: an upturned crown of eggshell, heaped with garlic cloves pierced with rosemary quills. Harmless kitchen sorcery; and yet, I am surprised at how this annoys me.

The morning of Erev Shabbat finds me scrawling and oblivious. I have been restless all week. Seeking inspiration, I frequently directed Castor to move my writing table about the villa. This morning, I am concealed too well.

Pollux and Arsinoë are absorbed in sexual horseplay, and stumble into my sanctuary behind the potted palms in the paristylium. Arsinoë's housedress is stripped to her waist, and Pollux fumbles with his girdle-band. Arsinoë shrieks when she sees me dipping my reed in the inkpot, regarding them wryly. Rigid with shock, Arsinoë then turns and pummels Pollux, curses him in Egyptian, and runs off in tears. He is left standing alone, looking culpable and foolish.

He says, "My Lord, please don't misunderstand … nothing was intended …"

"I would like some wine and refreshment now, Pollux, if that wouldn't be too much trouble." I struggle to mask amusement as I visualize my mission to purge the household of paganism, but then an idea comes to me.

"When Arsinoë has composed herself," I say. "I need to speak to you both."

Pollux stammers, "As … as you wish, my Lord."

These days I take my meals at my desk while I work. Before Castor sets down my tray, I ask him to move my writing table into the main courtyard where I resettle myself and eat while I review my latest entries. I presume I am being watched from one of the interior rooms because as soon as I push the food aside Pollux and Arsinoë reappear.

My former concubine is now barefoot and repentant. She has changed into a mourner's shroud and has shed her jewelry. Her lavish hair is pulled back into a knot at the base of her neck. I think she would have smeared her face with ashes if she'd had time. Sexless, she looks as though she has just detached from a funeral procession. She stands awaiting judgment, eyes downcast and hands clasped in front of her.

I set aside my writing instruments and clear my throat. "I am announcing changes which will affect the entire household. I have tolerated your use of magic, your traditional Heka." I see their alarm and hear their collective intake of breath. "Though venerable, it cannot coexist with Jewish law. I am master of this house and a Jew. From this day forward, this will be a Jewish household."

Pollux, wringing his hands, begins to kneel. "Master, Arsinoë and I meant no harm!" Seeing me motion for him to stand, he pleads: "It is just that you have seemed so removed, so distracted. You are neglecting yourself, abstaining from …" He raises Arsinoë's face by the chin, and she looks demure. "… your

Master's prerogative. We fear you are unwell. We have knowledge of so many curative remedies from home. We know the gods would favor you if we just make the correct offering."

"I appreciate your concern," I say, "but please, what I propose will benefit us all. Are you familiar with Jewish law?"

Their faces blank, they stare back at me.

"Never mind. I wish to begin the weekly observance of the Sabbath—now—at sundown tonight."

They exchange looks. Pollux asks, "What will you require of us, my Lord?"

"Your cooperation and companionship. Our first business is to plan a Seder. It is forbidden to kindle a fire or perform any work during Shabbat. So we will need to start organizing immediately."

Arsinoë interrupts, forgetting her recent disgrace. "Who is to cook and serve this banquet, Master? None of us is skilled in the kitchen to prepare such a feast."

"A Shabbat meal need not be grand, and since it will have to be provided out of food in supply here, it will certainly not be a banquet. Its chief purpose is to demonstrate gratitude to God for sustenance and for the love and companionship of family." Pausing, I break the awkward silence and add, "That is, if we wish to live more as a family."

My Egyptians still make no response. I continue: "You ask who will prepare the Seder? I am considering the milking overseer's wife, Lucretia."

Arsinoë staggers in disbelief. "A common field hand, working in our kitchen? Master, how could you?"

"She is a skillful cook for the vine-workers, and she has raised six healthy children. Her rustic Italian style will do us proud."

Castor reappears. He hands Pollux a scroll with a tabellarii seal, the mark of the slave-courier service. Pollux passes the message to me, and says, "My Lord, you say that all must put aside their labor for Shabbat. What of the vine-workers? Must the grape harvest suffer?"

"The grape harvest is in God's hands."

I unroll the message. It is from Patrolicus.

Bad news, my friend. Wagon delivering wine press equipment attacked and ransacked at Milestone XIII, Via Praeneste. Equipment destroyed. Gladiator guards deserted. All is lost.

I look up in amazement. "God has spoken. All will rest on Shabbat."

Un Marché á Tunis
Mark W. McIntire

Among baubee and bauble
Un beau coq I met.
Tumblers of tea leaves
Released ambrosia
As we volubly gibed
Trivial topics du jour.

A mouthpiece proffered
To puff the calabash.

We sipped and drew
Among the throngs
Of foreign tourists
In search of trinkets
From Berber markets
Filled with characters
Comme nous.

Finding Grace in the Absurd
An Interview with Gina Ochsner

Gina Ochsner's novel *The Russian Dreambook of Colour and Flight* (Houghton Mifflin Harcourt) came out in 2010. Her story collection *The Necessary Grace to Fall* (University of Georgia Press, 2002) won the Flannery O'Connor Award for Short Fiction and the Oregon Book Award. Her short story collection *People I Wanted to Be* (Mariner Books, 2005) also won the Oregon Book Award. She teaches in Seattle Pacific University's low-residency MFA program and at Corban University in Salem.

Tell us how your novel came about.

I thought that I was going to write a series of travel postcards with recipes on the back of different foods from Siberia.

I really thought that's what I was going to do. After traveling about and collecting recipes—or not collecting recipes, because no one can agree what the perfect borscht is made of. Do you put carrots in, or no carrots? That can divide a community—I realized I just don't know enough about this. I still think it's an interesting concept. But I wanted to try to go at something set in Russia in a different kind of a way. I liked the idea of this architecture where a story's not carried on the back of one character, or one theme, but several. It might be the short story writer in me that thinks like that. So that's why it's architected in the way that it is. It's four main characters each telling their own stories. And sometimes the stories overlap and sometimes they don't. Which is the way that life works, I think.

How would you describe the novel?

I would describe this as a post-Soviet, near-apocalyptic, magic-realist love story. And somebody reading this might think, "Love story? I don't see any love in

87

here." But I see the action of grace on each of the characters in some measure, and the presence of place as a character upon which the action of grace is also tangibly experienced.

It's satiric too, right?

I think it's totally absurd! I think getting fired on a little postage-size slip with no ink is totally absurd, but that could also really actually happen in Russia. It's that kind of a place. A friend was telling me, he had a book accepted for publication in Romania and then he got an e-mail saying, whoops, the publisher has run out of ink; we can't publish anything for two years. Who runs out of ink? But it happens. So I think of it as completely absurd. Somebody reading for profound truths might be disappointed, from time to time. And I can't do anything about that.

This novel is set in Russia, and a number of your short stories are also set in Eastern Europe. Do these places strike a chord with you?

I'm really drawn to those places. And it's very strange, absurd even, because I'm not Slavic, Baltic, Balkan, any of those things. So it's like falling in love with someone and somebody asking you, "Why did you fall in love with them anyway? What do you see in them?" How do you explain it? You just fall in love with things. You just do. And I have.

I'm really curious about the way other people make sense out of their world and the way they articulate their experience: their loss, their joy, their belief, their faith, their disappointment. And it is articulated differently in different cultures. There was a woman in Latvia. I went to a little church and she was probably 80 and she wanted everyone to pray for her. She stood up and she said, "All of my life's troubles would be solved if only I could have six more potatoes." You wouldn't hear that here. So that's why I travel; I want to hear, how do people put things into their own words? How is the body of belief carried on them tangibly? And what people hope for and wish for from place to place is by and large the same. We all want the best for our children, we all want peace in the world. But then there are these other things, like six potatoes. Or, "A little bit of baling wire would make all the difference." Wow, there's a story there.

Was this the first novel you've written?

It's the first novel that's been published. I have two languishing in a drawer. They'll stay in the drawer. I look at them and I say, "You sloppy, miserable mess, you. I learned so much from having written you, but the world will never see you and I'm so glad." It's like anything else, you have to write some horrible things before something comes together.

How did this novel come together? Had you spent most of your time with short stories?

Yeah, but what I did was, there was one story—it ended in a totally fine place, but it just seemed in my mind these characters are really kind of interesting. I wonder what would happen if each of them had a little more air time and we just sort of kicked the walls out on that story and allowed for some additions. That story is called the "Fractious South," in which there is a character who loves to fish—it's all he can think about—and his mother works at a newspaper. So I just started tinkering around with them, and found that if I gave each of them their own point of view, their own voice, those were two characters that just had a lot more to say. And then introducing somebody like Tanya came easy once the idea of putting everybody in the same collapsing building occurred. Then I populated the story with more absurd people and situations. It started with a short story, and like a kid with a peice of taffy, I kept pulling at it.

You teach in the Seattle Pacific University program. Do you recommend MFA programs?

I do. I highly recommend them. The famous quote from Flannery O'Connor, when asked if MFA programs stifle writers, is that' in her estimation the programs don't stifle enough of them. But she was grumpy, so we have to forgive her

I love teaching for the low-residency MFA because the premise is that this is the model for what your life would be like as a working writer afterward. You work, you have your family, you have your job, you have responsibilities, but you find ways to write around that. There's something kind of artificial—not bad, but kind of artificial—about the traditional two-year program where you uproot, you go, relocate, keep these studio hours, and you're supposed to be churning out things like a gerbil on a treadmill. But that's not real life.

Nobody can make somebody a good writer, even if they tried to open up all the doors to publishing. Good writing happens when the writers attends him or herself fully to the craft of writing. That's just hard work and nobody can do it for them. And that's such a downer of a thing to say. Because everybody wants the code. "Give me the secret. Is it wearing purple socks on Tuesday? I'll do it! Tell me how to do it." It's simply putting the butt in a chair for seven years, studying craft, reading the masters. How did Flaubert do that? Why did Chekhov write the way that he does? Why do we say these four-page stories changed the way writers think about writing? Why is he the grandfather of short stories? What makes Flannery O'Connor absolutely unforgettable? You have to study that style, that voice. And that can't be done for the writer. They have to do it for him or herself. Eventually all that work shows in what they're able to produce on their own, in their own voice, their own architectures.

Those people who are 21 and they publish and they're geniuses, they're really the freaks of nature and we can't look at them as the normative model. For the rest of us, it's hard work and time.

How would you say the Willamette Valley or the community of writers here has impacted your writing?

Greatly. I don't think anything of mine would be published if not for all the writers in the area with whom I meet, usually once a month. They mean everything to me. They are beyond mere friends, mere writers. They are kindred spirits, really. We've been at it for twelve years. One fella has been a long-haul trucker and writes poetry. He's not driving, he's doing something else now. Another fella is a computer IT genius and writes brilliant young adult novels. Another woman has home-schooled four of her children and writes poetry. Because of her astonishing imagery, it's like the roof of my brain has just been pulled off. They have been the best readers, bar none, because they read so attentively and so carefully and so intelligently.

So I think a huge amount of any achievement or anything that's ever happened to me is because of a whole network of other people, who'd be embarrassed if I mention them by name because they feel they haven't done anything, but they've done everything.

What do you think we can do to make the local writing scene stronger?

There are marvelous events hosted at the Salem Public Library on a regular basis and every third Thursday, Third Thursday Poets meet in the Reed Opera House. No doubt there are a boatload of other literary events occurring in the Salem area of which I'm simply unaware. Still, I'm a big fan of the idea that students and faculty among various campuses and members of the community could all come together not only to celebrate art, but also to give something to the surrounding community. What about an all-city open-to-all-ages Poetry Slam? What about a you-tube mini-film face off? What if the entry fee were two canned food items for the Marion Polk Food Share? I'm very interested, too, in mentoring middle school and high school students in under-served high schools and home school situations. I think that's something that a lot of local writers could get involved with.

We could all get together and figure out how we can mentor these young people. Can we raise money to create workshops for them? Create a place where they can work with somebody who's really good and teach them a few things about writing?

Incidentally, I'm in charge of putting together a writing conference next June at Corban. Jane Kirkpatrick and Diane Glancy are coming. And we're doing free workshops for high schoolers and middle schoolers.

On your Web site you offer talks and workshops on a number of things, including flash fiction and prose poetry. Do you write a lot of that?

It's a lot of fun. It forces me to think very, very hard about what makes a story a story. Stories can be told in 150 words, it's just hard. That's where I go back to Chekhov, to see how he wrote with complex compression.

It's a good genre too for magical realists. Because when we get tired, just flip out the lights, the story's done.

Any tips for magical realism? Is it hard to do?

I don't think it's hard to do. I think it's fun. To me it's the most fun thing in the world, and natural as breathing. But if somebody wants to know, how do I do this, I would say, read Kelly Link. And just try to think of the strangest, goofiest, wackiest situation, and write as if it were really happening. Don't make it somebody's dream and then they woke up and it was all a nightmare. No, it was really happening. With magical realism you have to go all the way and write risky territory.

Is there anything else you'd like to mention?

I'm really interested in Alpine yodeling lessons, if anybody wants to tell me about that. That's the best part of research.

Mark Russell Reed
Editor

Two Prophets
Mark Russell Reed

A man with a long white beard paced the city sidewalk ranting—though prophesying was the term he preferred. He wore a sandwich board sign that declared, "The World Will End Today." It was a bold statement, to be sure, but it set him apart from those who merely promised, "The End Is Near." Passersby largely ignored him, as only big city residents can, but he was occasionally yelled at, laughed at, or spat on. This he'd always been able to shoulder; he felt he was prophet and martyr both, even if both titles remained premature. In any event, he was willing to suffer for the word.

He ranted whether or not anyone was paying attention, or was even nearby, but he naturally preferred high-traffic areas. As things began to slow, he moved on to find a larger audience. He arrived at one of his favorite locations to find someone already there predicting imminent doom, a gray-bearded man whose sign stated, "The World Will End Tomorrow."

He was shocked at the man's audacity, but he wouldn't take it quietly. "The world will end TODAY!" he cried out, announcing his presence.

The gray-bearded prophet was startled, but quickly regained his composure. He increased his volume, but wouldn't rise to yelling. Not yet. "Tomorrow is the day! It has been ordained. The signs—"

"There will be no tomorrow! Repent now! Do not wait!"

They moved closer, addressing their rants directly to each other, oblivious to the passersby, who for the first time were taking a great interest. Soon the prophets were face-to-face, both screaming. The white-bearded prophet, gesturing wildly, accidentally made physical contact. The gray-bearded prophet shoved him in response. Perceiving that the line of physical contact had been crossed, the gray-bearded prophet shoved the white-bearded prophet in response. Then the sandwich boards came off and they started swinging.

If a significant aspect of religious belief is orientation toward time, these two were on the cutting edge, the very front lines. Out there together, they'd seem to the rest of us all but identical. But to themselves, side by side in the trenches, well, what a difference a day makes...

Two patrolmen pulled the prophets apart, to the crowd's dismay. "Now what's this about?" they asked.

"Today!"

"Tomorrow!"

"Today!"

"Tomorrow!"

The prophets lunged for each other, and were again restrained.

"It seems to be a theological dispute," a bystander said, indicating the sandwich board signs on the ground.

"Can't you find some sort of compromise?" someone else asked.

"If my sign said the day after tomorrow, I'd say we could definitely split the difference," the gray-bearded prophet said.

"Oh, that's clever," said the white-bearded prophet, sarcastically.

"Just go home," said the patrolmen. "You go that way, and you go that way. If we see you two together again today, you'll both be arrested."

"We'll see who's laughing tomorrow!" the gray-bearded prophet yelled out as a parting shot.

"There won't be a tomorrow!" the white-bearded prophet yelled back.

The white-bearded prophet went home. He listened to the evening news with his usual sense of disgust, then drifted off to sleep. He awoke late in the morning. The world was still there. No big deal; it had happened many times before. But then he remembered the other prophet. He knew the gray beard would be waiting for him. The general public he could face, but not that guy. That was personal.

Could he wear his "Today" sign as he always did? To wear it now would be moving into agreement with the "Tomorrow" sign from yesterday, essentially admitting the other guy was right. Yes, the end was nigh, and it was time to relinquish earthly attachments, but he still had his pride.

The gray-bearded prophet woke to as bright a dawn as he could remember. The world hadn't ended yesterday, so that other guy was wrong, just as he'd said. He couldn't wait to go out and spread the word of imminent destruction.

His sign had read, "The World Will End Tomorrow," every day. But just this once he'd make an exception—this day his sign would proclaim, "The World Will End Today." Just so the white-bearded prophet wouldn't have anything to use when he rubbed his false prediction in his face. His line of work granted few victories; he wouldn't let this one pass without exploiting it to the fullest.

He went out bright and early, an uncommon pep to his step. He had to keep back a grin that kept wanting to form on his lips. This excitement added a new dynamic to his voice, and people paid attention to him in greater numbers than ever. Maybe he'd have an actual crowd of listeners when the white-bearded prophet showed up. It couldn't be better.

He kept more mobile than usual. He didn't want to miss the white-bearded prophet if he did dare show his face. Would he even have the guts to appear? What would his attitude be? Humble and repentant? Bitter and angry? Embarrassed and ashamed?

Then his wait was over—he saw the white bearded prophet in the distance. He quickened his step and raised his voice a notch. There was his moment.

The white-bearded prophet was standing on a corner, pretending not to notice his opponent. When he got to within a few paces, the white-bearded prophet turned to face him. The gray-bearded prophet stopped short, suddenly flustered. He'd imagined plenty of things to say, but now that he could read the sign, he was nearly struck dumb.

"The World Ended Yesterday," it said.

"You ... you can't do that!"

"Do what?" asked the white-bearded prophet, feigning ignorance.

"Your sign. You can't preach that."

"I'm not preaching. What would be the point?"

"It's ridiculous! It makes no sense!"

The white-bearded prophet shrugged. Though hampered by the sandwich board, the gesture was effective—the gray-bearded prophet got so frustrated he lost all powers of articulate speech. Eventually he managed to get out, "Damn you!"

The white-bearded prophet turned and casually walked away. Tomorrow would find them on equal footing again. He looked forward to it.

Yesterday's News
Nyla Alisia

Rosehips
Brigitte R. C. Goetze

Bereft of its pink petals
the wild rose pistil persists,
an unlit candle.

Oh, how long the nights
which round and ripen
a red glow!

That lovely, fragile hope
of a second emergence,
engendered during the first flowering:

a fall filled
with luminous lanterns,
lasting all winter.

Eskimo Kiss
M.S. Ebbs

Even as I hold you and say the words I've said so many times before, I wonder how to make them fresh like snowflakes melting on the tongue. With all that familiarity, how can we keep things new? There are days when I feel the flutter of uncertainty like slipping across a layer of ice. Sometimes I struggle to remember that with all your idiosyncrasies, I'd still choose you. Other days are as real to me as the embrace of an arctic breeze. Still, I search for the perfect words, a meaningful look, something to say that after all these years I'd do everything again. Then when I've forgotten to try, forgotten to remember how, you touch the tip of your nose to mine and I know you feel the same way.

Love Sucks
cc: Mary Howitt
Heather Cuthbertson

Come a little closer, says the spider to the fly, for I am so lonely and in need of a friend. I won't hurt you. Look I'll stay right here on the other side of the web. I won't move any closer if only you'll talk to me. Please talk to me; it's been too long since I've had the company of another.

I haven't moved one bit, little fly. See, not one bit at all and you're right over there, stepping along the threads. You're not scared of me are you? You can see that I'm good on the inside. You can see I'm so much more than this body. So much more than my cursed nature, but that I have a heart and a soul. You can see that, can't you?

Come a little closer, says the spider to the fly, for I can tell you understand me and I want to understand you. Tell me your deepest thoughts and your grandest dreams, and I'll tell you mine. Let's spin a new world with only us, just us, because nobody understands like we do, feels like we do, and hopes like we do.

Don't go away, little fly, I only moved just a pinch. I promise I won't come any closer. You mustn't be afraid. We have a connection, you and I. Can you feel it? It hums along these very threads, weaving and crossing and winding and coiling. It's like a dance. A marvelous, miraculous dance. Oh dear, I accidentally took another step. I didn't mean anything by it. Really, I didn't. My happiness overtook me and I've been waiting so long for a moment just like this one, just like this.

Come a little closer, says the spider to the fly, for I need someone to trust and I've been hurting for so long. I need to feel you next to me. I need to know that I'm not alone. You're all I've ever wanted. Can't you see how much I care? How special you are? If I hurt you, then I'd only be hurting the deepest part of myself. You know that, don't you? In your heart, you have to know that.

Do you feel as I do, little fly? I'm ready for so much more and I hope, only a little, that maybe, just maybe you feel the same. Please tell me you do. Whisper it if you must. I'll lean in closer so you can, just don't back away from me. You'll make me cry if you do. It's just one step closer, a slight movement, and I feel so drawn to you. I can't resist. Something is pulling us together. Can't you feel it? Tell me you can. Say that you can.

Come a little closer, says the spider to the fly, for I need and crave you. You are all that I've ever wanted, all that I've dreamed of. Don't you feel the same? You must or you wouldn't be so near, so close, I could almost touch … Oh but I won't, I promise. Unless you want me too. Do you? I cannot deny that I desire you. It's all I can think about it; it occupies my every thought. Let me show you how much I love you.

Don't you love me, little fly? Say that you do. I need to hear it for I've been so lonely and in need of a friend. I'll do anything to make you happy. Anything at all because that's how true my feelings are for you. Give me a chance. That's all I'm asking. One, small chance and you'll see how tender my love is.

Come a little closer, says the spider to the fly, for you're the most beautiful thing I've ever seen, so beautiful that you can't possibly be real. If I could touch you for simply a moment, then I would know that you are. Allow me one caress. Please, just one. That's all I ask. I can't help myself much longer. I'm trying to fight it, but something inside me wants you madly.

Don't move away, little fly. I can see you trembling. We're so close now. I can see the lines of your gossamer wings. I'll drape them in silk and we'll watch them sparkle like diamonds within diamonds. They are so enchanting; my lips yearn to brush against them. One kiss and I can live happily with just having the memory of feeling you, feeling—oh, don't go. Please don't go. I only touched them for a second, only for a second. That's all I needed. Really.

Come a little closer, says the spider, to the fly, for I fear you're going to leave me. You'll go away just like all the others. Can't you see how my heart is breaking? You're already turning away and I don't know how I can live without you now that we've been so close.

Don't leave me, little fly. Tell me what I've done wrong and I'll fix it. I'll do anything. Don't leave me all alone. I will die without you. Surely, I will. I will draw myself into a little ball and wait for death to come. Can't you see that life has no meaning for me without you? Stay just a moment longer. That's all I ask. Stay.

Come a little closer, says the spider to the fly, for we should be together, forever and ever and ever. We can if you'll surrender yourself to me, surrender completely. I can tell you want this as much as I. You wanted too the moment you set upon my web. Don't deny it. It was meant to be. I knew you'd come to me. I always knew.

Don't be frightened, little fly. See how gentle I am? See how my touch is full of care, wrapping you in a cocoon of love, little by little. Bit by bit. Almost done. Let me stand back and see. Ah, there you are. So beautiful, so bewitching. I can hardly constrain myself any longer. I want all of you, but I know I mustn't. I'll only hold you, very gently, very tenderly, while you sleep for a while. Sleep.

My love.

You're so still.

Nonfiction Love
Joe Donovan

I'm in love with someone in my creative nonfiction class and I like salt. Trust me. But liking salt and loving her are difficult to do together. Eating too much salt makes my stomach hurt. When my stomach hurts, I can't do much else but think about my hurting stomach. Yes, salt can distort my day and can hyperbolize everything.

It's not because her hair is nice or because her stride is bouncy that makes her attractive. It's not because she has good ideas or witty comments or because she has nice handwriting. I like salt because it's not sweet. I love her because raindrops collected in a cup are always surprisingly brown even when individual drops look clear. I love her for the same reason I like theories of deer and elk evolving from triceratops dinosaurs. I love her because messy spills, like oil spills, create beautiful sunsets. Here is why one person in my creative nonfiction class makes my heart burst.

Wednesday: It's raining and I'm working. My clothes are wet. I can feel the April raindrops move down my neck and enter the area under my shirt where my skin is white. Despite the cold, I feel warm. I'm in a Salem parking lot and today is my dad's birthday. I work for a sorority. I work for a bunch of women. I clean yogurt out of shiny bowls and wipe lipstick off the rims of dinner glasses with shiny Greek letters. There is always so much sparkle in this house.

I'm searching for significance.

I feel fuzzy and I'm happy. I should be cold. I should be miserable. I watch friends, faceless by giant parkas, march through the weather with hunched shoulders. They look at me and smile.

I wish I could get to the bottom of who is leaving the trash bags outside the dumpster. That is my job, but I can't stop thinking about her. How do I speak to this sensation? I want to dance. I should be freezing.

If today were Friday, I'd be unhappy. But today is Wednesday, which means yesterday was Tuesday and I'm riding an intoxicating infatuation. Today is Wednesday and I'm in love with someone in my creative nonfiction class.

Out here in the rain next to the blue dumpster I think about Tuesday and Thursday mornings. On those mornings I wake up singing the same song. There's a halo hanging from the corner of my girlfriend's four-post bed. The song should be called "Tuesday and Thursday Mornings." This is true because this is nonfiction.

I think about how the sorority dumpster allows me to find significance. By significance I mean something that credits my Tuesday/Thursday Love. I start with my location. I'm standing next to the dumpster. The dumpster serves the three sororities on campus. It's a generic blue color and is large enough to hold WEEKS of trash. A pink shape, weeks old, has become a permanent fixture on the side of the dumpster. It's composed of makeup and strawberry yogurt. There is so much makeup and yogurt in this dumpster.

Does she like yogurt?

I've learned to hop over the stand-alone garbage bag. I anticipate the stinging nasal sensation that accompanies the miniature bacteria devouring the banana carcasses. I focus on the pretty yogurt stain on the side of the dumpster. These things are important because I'm writing creative nonfiction.

This is what happens when you're in love like I am.

The trash sits outside the dumpster. The makeup and yogurt stain above the bag. Together, it looks like a juicy blackberry with a pink stem.

Sag marks of garbage connect our "service entrance" with the problematic trash bags. It looks like a translucent leech. I see this garbage-paste-connection as a signifier of my love and my inherent connection to her. I imagine an A on one end and a B on the other. If I'm A and she is B, then together our love is signified by a glowing line of garbage paste. This is love. I try to think about garbage but yesterday was Tuesday and tomorrow is Thursday.

Today is Wednesday. I'm sandwiched by love days.

Sunday: It's cloudy but I don't mind. In two days it's Tuesday. I sit with a large college kid wearing a baseball hat with "Got Milk" stitched across the bill. I want to wear his hat. Instead, I watch his mouth move. We're the same age, this kid and I, but I call him a kid because he dresses like a little leaguer.

Does she like yogurt?

If I wear his hat, I will look like a dairy farmer. I've been told farm boys catch girls. Farm boys aren't scared to use real leeches. They don't need leeches made from garbage paste. But this sounds weird and I don't really love "Got Milk" hats.

He's pointing to a gray streak on his computer. "Are you listening?" he asks.

I pay attention because she would think he's funny.

Some weekend night, which by nature is two or three days away from Tuesday, he was drinking with friends in his dorm room.

Joe Donovan

"Then I was like, shit," he tells me, tipping his cap slightly, "there was a knock on my door. Campus Safety was trying to bitch us out."

I believe him because Campus Safety is pathetic.

"I go to hide the booze," he tells me, his eyes moving from left to right, "but knock one over onto my computer."

I believe this too because dorm rooms aren't designed for farm animals.

I imagine the mess of brown ale spilling over his little black plastic computer keys. His screen must have looked intoxicated.

"BALLS. The only thing I could do then was to get the Febreze to cover the smell of beer. I grabbed the spray and the nozzle was loose then 'fresh spring morning' spilled over my computer too."

I know how the computer feels. I, too, am intoxicated by fresh spring mornings.

The mixture of brown ale and Febreze brought me back to Wednesday at the dumpster where the trash bag and the sweet yogurt stain reminded me of her. Messes remind me of Tuesdays and Thursdays. I like the idea of catastrophic spills having a lot of ingredients. Today is Sunday and I'm 48 hours away from Tuesday.

This is what she is like. This is why I love her: In class she'll say something like, "I love the ambiguity of this piece but I'm not sure what it's about." Her voice is lighter and resonates nicely in the stuffy classroom. "I guess," she'll continue, "I really was looking for more clarity."

I'm never sure what she'll say. Sometimes she talks a lot, other times she's quiet. I can't tell if what she says is actually true. Does she actually like ambiguity or does she like to mix compliments with critiques?

What could I say if I had a larger vocabulary? I could mix words like quasi and meta with other large words and she'd be impressed. Maybe I could drip into my locution smart phrases from different languages like French or Latin. I could say, "The dénouement really established this piece as meta-nonfiction." But really you'd have to take my words with a grain of salt because I don't know what I'm saying. Trying to impress her through language is silly.

And she will not believe my words because language is silly. She knows this. Words are only half-truths.

Maybe, when she reads this, she'll critically analyze this essay. She'll ask objectively. "To whom is he writing this? Whom does he love?" She'll use "whom" because she always sounds smart and smart people use "whom." She's smart because she is levelheaded and she told me once that her GPA is higher than 3.0.

I'm not telepathic, so I shouldn't waste time thinking about what other people are thinking. And I shouldn't waste time with fancy jointed words like telepathic. I should think about my GPA.

Tuesday: Today is Tuesday and yesterday I spilled yogurt on the carpet. The rich color clung to the furry strands like paintbrush thistles. I added a few pinches of salt. I looked at the pink abstraction on the floor and thought by adding salt I was making this giant mess significant.

Water Soluble
Bethany Williams

Other scenes, eerily similar, sail in through pores opened by hot water. We've been here so often before, seen each other in the yellow light, smelled the lavender soap and peppermint shampoo on one another. Desire fulfilled and minds relieved, we pay attention to our tired bodies. The excitement of fresh intimacy, ease of companionship, and after-fight enmity soaked and scrubbed pink. The smells, sights, and sensations in the watery, two-foot box are all the same, but these particular vapors are exceptional.

My chin rests in the water running off his ears and into the bowl between his collarbone and neck. A liquid staccato massages my skin but my muscles stay tense and my lungs tight. I don't want this. We never imagined this version of finality, but this is where it ends. We cling to each other, grasping tightly even as we are rinsed away with the suds. Compressed thighs and chests sway left and right. My tepid tears and his silence express our futility.

We rouse ourselves. I turn away and breathe into the current while he busies himself with soap and shampoo. An impish gleam replaces the heaviness in his eyes and the hand that holds my waist grabs my wrist, lifting my arm into the air. He smirks at the slow realization making its way across my face.

I feign refusal, but a telltale grin spurs him on. He begins with my most sensitive places and sings as he lathers my unwilling underarm. Though I squirm, I am grateful for this routine silliness. I watch his singing mouth and I smile as soap froths, lathering down my sides and sliding over the transition between round and linear found at the top of each of my thighs. Every point learned and savored in repetition. I know this feeling; we've been here.

Relief rushes over our heads and down our bodies. I indulge in his willingness to entertain and we move away from reality and back to lavender. I look into green eyes, widened by song and rimmed with lashes bundled into tiny paintbrushes. We dance in a tight circle, moving around each other and reciting familiar verses of "your turn" and "I need to rinse," while avoiding the curtain; its shocking coolness threatening our sanctuary.

I turn the water off, cold nozzle and then hot. By the time I wring out my hair, he's already wrapped in a towel and holding mine open. I back into it and he rubs it around my back, drying and enveloping me like a parent after a young child's swimming lesson. My chin finds that perfect ravine between his throat and shoulder, and the rivulet running his neck trickles between my parted lips. We allow ourselves a few drippy seconds and then open the door.

Middle School Sway
Danny Earl Simmons

we dance
a very adult
middle school sway
in the shower, gently
rocking this way then that
way, body pressed firmly into
body, eagerly kissing, eagerly caressing,
determined to make urgent use of this most
unexpected opportunity for steam and sweat,
chance for primal reminder of our love that made our
awake
again
baby
boy.

Conversations with My Mother's Purse
F.I. Goldhaber

The phone jangles with their special ring.
I answer, hear her distant voice, but
can't make out her words. Thinking it a
bad connection, I hang up and call
back. No response. Now, I worry. Has
my father taken ill again? I
learn later, all is well. She had stuck
her earpiece in her purse, it turned on,
and re-dialed the last number called.

When it happens again, I hear the
unmistakable background beep of
medical monitoring machines.
This time I get an answer when I
call back. "Yes, Dad's in the hospital.
He may have had a heart attack, but
he's doing fine now." She'd planned to call
soon, to let me know. I wonder when
did the spirits start using cell phones?

One Snowy Night
Sandra M. McDow

She rested, immobile, slumped in her seat-sprung, frayed recliner, chin on her chest, snorting an occasional sleep sound. Except for an intermittent soft snore, she could be dead. Her dry, wrinkled face was slack and unmoving except for the occasional twitch of her lips, as if she were smiling at some inner joke. Outside, the snow fell.

"Chirp. Chirp, chirp."

She started in her sleep and then opened lid-crusted eyes. What had she heard? There, there it was again. "Chirp. Chirp, chirp." She shook her head, rearranging an unkempt halo of silver hair, rubbed her eyes and the small bit of drool from the side of her mouth. She cocked her head, pink and scaly scalp catching the light and shining through her thinning hair, and then slowly rose from the chair to move cautiously and watchfully around the room. Nothing. After the slow reconnoiter, she moved, joints popping and cracking, toward the murky window by the front door. With her fingers, she wiped the moisture off the glass, creating a peephole to view the tiny, tilted porch and dirty patch of snow beyond. Dark sky, light snow, no birds. Not there! Where, then—in the house?

Oh! It stopped. She shook her head and returned to the chair, which received her with the familiarity of a lover, molding itself to her back, buttocks and legs as if she had never left. She pulled an old afghan over her legs, leaned her head back and resumed her nap. Her eyes twitched, then her body jerked as she uttered a phlegmy sigh, signaling her return to oblivion.

"Chirp. Chirp, chirp." The high-pitched sounds resonated through the three cluttered rooms. Sleep-stunned, she arose painfully and began myopically scanning the corners, ceilings, floors, and furniture as she moved from room to room. Nothing. Standing at the kitchen counter, she picked up the smudged telephone receiver with one liver-spotted hand while she fumbled with her dog-eared address book with the other, tearing the page she was trying to peruse. She exchanged the receiver for the magnifying glass lying beside the telephone. Magnifier in hand, she studied the torn page and then voiced the ten-digit number aloud while carefully placing a knobby index finger into each numbered hole in the dial.

"Chirp. Chirp, chirp."

"Hurry up and ring," she muttered. The moment the answering machine activated, she began talking "Son! I have a bird in the house. I can't find it. It might be a bat—they carry rabies you know—can you come?" No answer. She replaced the receiver, disconnecting just as the machine signaled its readiness to record.

She paced the worn linoleum floors, finally returning to the front window. Outside, snowfall deepened the darkness of early nightfall; there were no cars moving on the street and no sign of another living soul. Who would come out on a night like this anyway? With a sigh, she turned from the window, crossed her arms over her withered breasts, and while rubbing her upper arms with open palms, shook her head slowly and entered the bedroom.

Cold. She lit the open-faced gas heater and turned back the thick, stained feather comforter on the bed. As she edged close to the heater, she pulled her raveled sweater over her head, and shrugged into a thin flannel nightgown. Still cold. Shoulder joints popping their complaint, she pulled the sweater back over her head and smoothed it over the top of the worn gown. Then, she slipped out of her snagged polyester pants, and left them in a crumpled pile at her feet. She just needed to get warm.

"Chirp. Chirp, chirp."

Lying in her feathery nest under the thick, stained comforter, she wiggled her feet seeking relief from its pressure on her bunions. She didn't hear the last, faint chirping sound as the smoke alarm battery finally died.

The room grew warmer. In the silence, she drifted off.

The room was almost still; the only discernable movements the dancing gas flame and the slow blistering of rumpled polyester as her pants began to smolder.

Sandra M. McDow

Their Song
Lois Rosen

One day I was listening to the AM radio as I parked in the home's lot. How many years had it been since I'd heard "a kiss is just a kiss, a sigh is just a sigh, the fundamental things apply, as time goes by?" I gripped the bumpy steering wheel till the song ended.

Sublimity, Oregon was no Yonkers and never would be. My father wasn't crooning the lyrics into a pretend mike, swaying and bending toward my mother sweating over a reeking pan of liver and onions. Her wavy hair no longer dipped in the front a la Lauren Bacall. In matched earrings, pearlized pop-it beads, and a frilly hand-embroidered apron she'd sewn herself, she was not in her kitchen, waving her spatula, telling him to get out of the way while she was cooking, and saying look out for the sizzling Crisco or they'd both get burned, when she couldn't help grinning or keeping her ample rear from swaying.

Through the windshield and a barbed wire fence, I watched black and white cows and calves standing beside each other chewing tufts of spring grass. The cows' bulk and the furriness of their hides surprised me, their eyelashes so long and dark, too, eyes the color of melted Hershey bars and that sweet-looking. The Oregon afternoon was warm enough I might wheel Mama out though what use would there be rolling her wheelchair to face those dumb beasts as she'd think of them?

This you call entertainment? her voice, that used to know how to form sentences, complained in my head. For Bossy the cow you dragged me to No Man's Land?

The instant I left the car, they began lowing and backing away and then running over the ridge no matter how much I wanted to assure them I meant no harm, hadn't eaten steak in years, that I longed to lay my cheek against their flanks, pretend they were the plush toys of my childhood, not that I'd ever played with a toy cow. And the truth be told, I was at that moment carrying a leather handbag and dragging myself into the Santiam home in loafers made from some member of their species even if the slaughter had occurred in Brazil.

Inside the white stucco building that once housed nuns, my Jewish mother appeared, thankfully, too demented to realize the home's former use. No matter how fluorescently lit, the corridor to reach her remained dim. In the Chinook Unit Room 113 was the woman who was supposed to be my mother, hag hair hanging like spent elastic, skinny sausage legs and arms encased in a pink sweat suit. The oxygen lines draped over her ears had shifted her glasses, so they rested mid-nose, useless. One of the plastic inserts from the breathing tube to her nostrils slanted down a quarter inch below where it was supposed to be.

"Hi, Mom. Nice to see you."

"Nice to see you," she echoed.

I leaned toward her on the big recliner, the kind that can hurl the body forward, and pushed the glasses and oxygen plug into place. Her eyes, the same hazel as mine, had less expression than the cows'. Asking her how she was, asking her about her day, asking her if she wanted to go outside, she looked through me. I nattered on about my work at the gallery, her grandson, Matt.

"Matt," she repeated in a monotone while her bony, dried hands picked at the afghan some church group had donated to the home. It didn't matter she'd made dozens herself.

I rang for the nurse's aide. My favorite, Rosie, worked that shift, but in came Nancy, the sub who didn't lotion mom's face, sit with an arm around her, or sing her lullabies the way Rosie did. Staff turned over constantly in this place. You never knew who'd show up or disappear.

"Where's Rosie?" I asked.

"Where's Rosie?" Mom said as spittle rolled out the side of her mouth. I wiped it away.

Nancy whispered, "Gone."

But Rosie had worked hard. "She took good care of my mother, a kind woman."

"Well, I didn't know her much. I gotta scurry." No hug for Mom, no extra tucking of the afghan.

I didn't want to be disappointed and not that I had much of a singing voice, but it had worked before. I started crooning our usual repertoire, "Home on the Range" first. When I got to the chorus, Mama sang "Home, home on the range" and chimed in with "all day." Her face brightened. Would she remember, "As Time Goes By?"

I began singing, "You must remember this, a kiss is just a kiss… as time goes by." Silence.

"Mama, remember Papa singing to you?" I kissed her hollow cheek. The skin felt cold. "A kiss," I said.

"A kiss," she mumbled it, but definitely the word.

"You must remember this, a kiss is just a kiss." I sang it alone. Her glasses slumped down again to the middle of her nose.

Traveling Companions
Mark W. McIntire

I travel with friends of different sizes
Many fat, others trim.
They wear worn tattered jackets
Appear brittle or jaundice skinned.
These friends tell great adventures
Valiant battles with fair maids to win.

They often travel in my pockets
Or sleep in bed beneath my chin.
You may want books much newer
Yet I am of a different ken.
I like them more if they are old
Replete with tales strong and bold.

Future
Nyla Alisia

Meet the Contributors

Nyla Alisia is both an award-winning poet and photographer. Her works can be found in numerous publications and websites worldwide. Nyla is the founder and host of three international poetry radio shows, The SpeakEasy Cafe, The Inkwell, and Re-verse. She also teaches creative vision photography and writing workshops.

Ariel, a Pacific Northwest Poet, has been published in several publications including print and online. She is a member of several organizations and is a board member of Third Thursday Poets. Ariel is a very active participant of the Open Mics and Spoken Word events in the Willamette Valley.

John Byrne lives in Albany. He writes short stories, short poems, and short plays for people and puppets. His work has appeared in *14 by 14, Lucid Rhythms, String-Town*, and many other print and internet journals as well as in the recent anthology of Northwest verse: *Many Trails to the Summit*.

Heather Cuthbertson has been writing for what feels like forever and generally has a few writing projects going at once. She is a graduate student at Antioch University, Los Angeles in their MFA program for Creative Writing.

Joe Donovan lives for second-hand cigarettes. He's not a smoker but he loves smoky discomfort intruding his lungs. He feels the same about writing. Today smoking and writing provide uncomfortable inspiration for expression. He lives in Salem and believes in good pictures that are embarrassingly personal.

M.S. Ebbs has been writing and studying the craft for over 20 years. She is the Willamette Writers Salem Chapter founder and Representative and is very active in the writing community. She is also a member of Romance Writers of America and has had success in RWA contests.

Stephen Eichner was born in Berkeley, California. He studied history at UCLA, and then worked as a law enforcement investigator. *T'shuvah* was first conceived while visiting Italy in 2001, and further inspired by travel in Israel in 2004. He will return to Italy in 2012 for three months of research.

Bob Gersztyn published his first article in 1996 in Duprees Diamond News, where he worked as a freelance photographer. Since then he has published hundreds of articles about music, religion, and other subjects in dozens of hard copy and electronic publications including *Blueswax*, *Statesman Journal*, and *The Wittenburg Door*, to name some.

Brigitte R.C. Goetze, biologist, goat farmer, writer, lives in the foothills of Oregon's Coast Range. She has been published by *Oregon Humanities*, *Quiet Mountain Essays*, *Thresholds*, *Outwardlink*, *Four and Twenty*, *Poets for Living Waters*, *Calyx*, *Women Artists Datebook 2011*, *Mused* and others.

F.I. Goldhaber is an editor, poet, novelist, story teller. She's written professionally for more than a quarter century and has had short stories, poems, news stories, features, essays, editorials, and reviews published in magazines, e-zines, newspapers, calendars, and anthologies as well as three erotica novels published under another name. www.goldhaber.net

Samuel Hall has been writing for the past 20 years. He is a member of Oregon Christian Writers, Willamette Writers, and American Christian Fiction Writers. He's shopping his novel and has had a number of articles, essays, and on-line pieces published.

Darren Howard was born in Los Angeles, and lived in Santa Cruz, Philadelphia, and Ypsilanti before settling in Salem, Oregon almost four years ago, as a Visiting Assistant Professor at Willamette University. His published works so far include several academic articles, in addition to his dissertation on the role of animals in British Romantic literature.

Marc Janssen is a graduate of California Lutheran University with a degree in Communications. A veteran of the nineties Ventura poetry scene, he has been published in a number of magazines and journals. Currently working for the State of Oregon, Janssen can be seen at open mics in the Salem area.

G.R. Vince Johnson, U.S. Navy 1945-1946 and 1950-1951. Successful Career in Marketing and Advertising. Played Chief Inspector Hubbard in "Dial M For Murder" produced by Theatre West in Lincoln City. Currently active in Aumsville Community Theatre. Wrote column known as "Reality Check" for *Silverton Appeal Tribune* and *Stayton Mail* for over three years.

Sandra McDow, learning disabilities specialist/consultant, holds B.S., M.S., and PhD degrees in related areas. She is currently enrolled in Pacific University's MFA writing program. She is a member of Willamette Writers and a Salem W.W. critique group.

Mark W. McIntire writes fiction and poetry in Salem where he enjoys life with his family and friends. He speaks on creativity, intercultural issues and faith while advocating for the appreciation of the arts in public life. He is currently working on a suspense novel and a screenplay.

Michael Pacheco debut novel, *The Guadalupe Saints*, was published in April 2011. His novella, *Seeking Tierra Santa*, was released in May 2011. He has two additional short stories to be published Fall 2011. Michael received his bachelor's degree from Gonzaga University and a law degree from Willamette University.

Melanie Patterson enjoys photography as a hobby. She is also a published writer and works as a Mental Health RN. Other hobbies include camping, biking, travel, reading, and being a mother.

Tim Pfau is a husband, father, grandfather who travels, reads, and writes full time. He serves on the Board of the Oregon Poetry Association. www.oregonpoets.org If sharing isn't the goal, why write it down?

Naseem Rakha is an award-winning author and journalist. Her novel, *The Crying Tree*, was the recipient of the 2010 Pacific Northwest Booksellers Association (PNBA) award. Naseem resides in Silverton, Oregon with her husband, son, and a whole bunch of animals.

Mark Russell Reed is a technical writer and editor for the world's largest technology company. He has a Bachelor of Arts from Wesleyan University, where he majored in philosophy, and is currently enrolled in the Atheneum master writing program at the Attic Institute in Portland. Visit markrussellreed.com and twitter.com/badpandas.

Nicklas Roetto, part human/part robot, was created in Redding, California before enlisting in the Air Force and completing a tour in Iraq. He recentlty installed a degree in Psychology from the University of Oregon and he is currently downloading his Masters in Business Administration at Marylhurst University. Nick loves spreadsheets.

Lois Rosen is a retired Chemeketa Community College ESL teacher who teaches writing at Willamette University. Traprock Books published her poetry book, *Pigeons*. Her stories and poems have appeared in numerous magazines including: *Willow Springs, Calyx, and Northwest Review*. She enjoys living in Salem with her husband and her cat, Pauline.

Jean Rover has worked as a freelance writer/editor and has an extensive background in corporate and marketing communications. She now writes fiction, personal essays and poetry. Her work has appeared in literary journals and the "This I Believe" project.

Kathleen Saviers, after working in law enforcement forensic sciences for more than thirty years, is changing careers to fiction writing. She has written three research papers published in scholarly journals and this is her first published short story. Currently, she is writing a police procedural novel involving forensics.

Danny Earl Simmons is a proud graduate of Corvallis High School and has loved living in the Mid-Willamette for over 30-years. He is a friend of the Linn-Benton Community College Poetry Club. He works for Knife River and currently serves on the Board of Directors of Albany Civic Theater.

Monica Storss is a poet, pedagogue, punk rock icon(oclast), performance artist, producer (Literary Death Match) and publicist. She holds an MFA from the University of California at Davis. She accepts love letters, dead butterflies, hummingbird skulls, peonies, dinner dates, walks on the beach, vagabonds, trainhoppers, music, and PR inquiries at monicastorss.org.

Isaiah Swan is a college undergraduate tentatively exploring the magical world of making things up for money. He has lived in Keizer, Oregon for the past 10 years and is currently studying English at Willamette University.

Bethany Williams, until she read, was not a writer. Writing was purely analytical until fate was altered and an English major with everything figured out became a student comfortable in her own bewilderment. Bethany Williams grew up in the desert, lives on the coast, and studies in the valley of Oregon.

Frank Yates, a former writer for a Fortune 500 company, now lives to ride Harleys, lives to write fiction, and lives in Stayton, Oregon. To live, he trades in the stock market. An active member of critique groups and writing organizations,

cogitate studios

BOOK EDITING & WRITING

OVER 100 EDITED TITLES IN PRINT

READER'S REPORTS,
COPYEDITING, PROOFREADING,
QUERY LETTERS, BOOK PROPOSALS,
DEVELOPMENTAL EDITING
& GHOSTWRITING

www.CogitateStudios.com

Tap into Expert Advice and Skill

Elizabeth Lyon ~ literary consultant, book editor, and author of 5 books on writing craft

- 1 hour Consultation, or
- 1 hour Critical Read-through, or
- 1 hour Edited Manuscript

**ELIMINATE FRUSTRATION
GET FOCUSED AND MOTIVATED
MAXIMUM RESULTS >> MINIMUM COST**

www.elizabethlyon.com   elyon123@comcast.net

1 Hour for $100

BOOK DARTS

Q: HOW CAN YOU HELP ALMOST ANY BOOK LOVER BECOME AN EVEN GREATER READER?

A: MAKE IT FAST AND EASY TO CAPTURE AND RECALL ANY LINE IN ANY BOOK!

"hold that thought"

"In a mushroom manual, a single Book Dart could save your life; in a cookbook, they'll just make sure you eat good." —Nate Dunn, Salem, OR

Join The Slow Reading Movement

Congratulations to The Gold Man Review from Book Darts!

It was endeavors like this that first inspired us to create **Book Darts** nearly twenty years ago (anyone remember **Left Bank** or **Mississippi Mud**?) Today, they continue to motivate us to be more deliberate and receptive in our reading, and most of all, to share the ideas we find.

Remember: None of us will ever read all the good stuff; we'll never even notice all that's good in what we do read. So, we need help in unlocking more of the treasures our books contain. Book Darts are one fine way to do this... with no harm to the page.

Helping Readers Grow, One Idea At A Time, Since 1992

www.bookdarts.com • info@bookdarts.com • 800-354-2230 • Hood River, OR

WILLAMETTE WRITERS

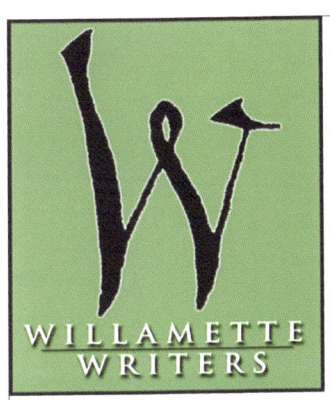

Join for only $36 per year!

- Monthly meetings with popular speakers
- Five chapter locations throughout Oregon - Portland, Salem, Eugene, Medford and Newport
- Annual writers conference - held August 3-5, 2012 - where you can pitch to agents, editors and producers
- Writing house for members' use
- Books for Kids & Young Willamete Writers
- Workshops, networking, critique groups...and more!

WILLAMETTEWRITERS.COM
WILWRITE@WILLAMETTEWRITERS.COM
503-305-6729

CLOCKWORKS
CAFE & CULTURAL CENTER
241 Commercial Street NE

Supporting the
Culture Shock Community Project
a 501(c)(3) non profit
www.clockworkscafe.com

Faith and Excellence in Writing since 1963

February 25, 2012	Winter One-Day Conference with **Lauraine Snelling** keynoting Red Lion Hotel, Salem
May 19, 2012	Spring One-Day Conference with **Karen Ball** keynoting Northwest Christian University, Eugene
August 13–16, 2012	Summer Coaching Conference with **Jim Rubart & Cecil Murphey** keynoting Aldersgate Retreat Center, Turner
October 13, 2012	Fall One-Day Conference with **Colleen Coble** keynoting Multnomah University, Portland

For details about Oregon Christian Writers programs and events, visit our website www.oregonchristianwriters.org

PDX Writers

Inspiring workshops for every writer
www.pdxwriters.com

- Great facilitators
- In-workshop writing
- Affordable pricing

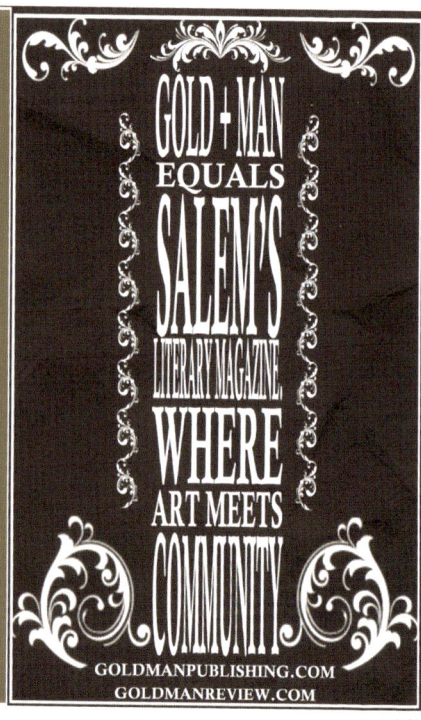

GOLD + MAN EQUALS SALEM'S LITERARY MAGAZINE, WHERE ART MEETS COMMUNITY

GOLDMANPUBLISHING.COM
GOLDMANREVIEW.COM

Advertisements

CPSIA information can be obtained
at www.ICGtesting.com
Printed in the USA
252629LV00001B